Out Into The Beautiful World

Also by Theodore Dalrymple from
New English Review Press:

Anything Goes (2011)

Farewell Fear (2012)

Threats of Pain and Ruin (2014)

Out Into The Beautiful World

Theodore Dalrymple

Published by New English Review Press
a subsidiary of World Encounter Institute
PO Box 158397
Nashville, Tennessee 37215
&
27 Old Gloucester Street
London, England, WC1N 3AX

Cover Art & Design by Kendra Mallock

ISBN: 978-1-943003-02-0

First Edition

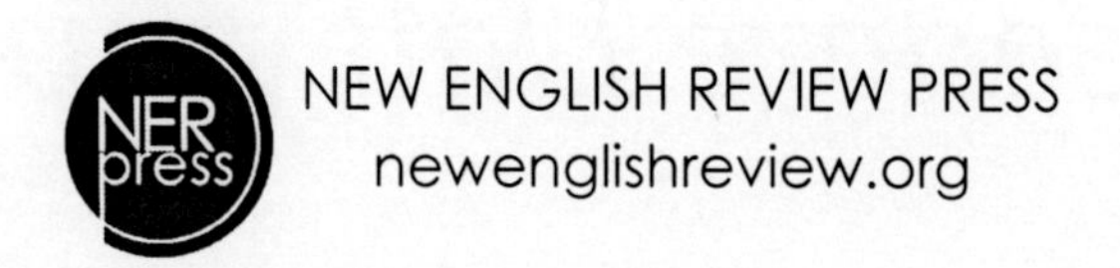

For my wife, Agnès

Carry me out
Into the wind and the sunshine
Out into the beautiful world.

—W E Henley, Discharged, Number XXVIII of the Hospital Poems (Henley was a patient of Joseph Lister in the Edinburgh Royal Infirmary for eighteen months. Lister saved his tuberculous leg from having to be amputated, as his other already had been).

Contents

Preface xi

1 - Apocalypse Now 13

2 - Destructive Creation 18

3 - What a Falling Prof. Was There 24

4 - A Game of Rat and Mouse 29

5 - Hitching to Gomorrah 35

6 - Eternal Youth, Eternal Kitsch 40

7 - What Dreams May Come 46

8 - Spider Man 51

9 - Serial Killers and Serial Explanations 56

10 - The Meaning of Life 61

11 - Zerbran at the Bozar 66

12 - Lunch Conquers All, Part I 71

13 - Lunch Conquers All, Part II 77

14 - How I Rwanda What You Are 82

15 - Driven Mad 88

16 - Fact and Tact 93

17 - Warmth is Cool 98

18 - Flying High 104

19 - Chinese Puzzles 110

20 - And Death Shall Have His Dominion 115

21 - A Battle of Algiers 120

22 - Of Chekhov, Dickens, Henley and Pascal 125

23 - And Some Have Greatness Thrust From Them 131

24 - Graves' Disease? 136

25 - Doing the Charleston 142

26 - Falstaff the Brave 147

27 - All Men Are Created Snobs 152

28 - Reading Your Stasi 158

29 - Sir Joshua and the Tumbling Walls 163

30 - Hazards of Hazlitt 169

31 - From Scotland to Timor 174

32 - Traviata Trivia 180

33 - Our Dreams Are Such Stuff As We Are Made On 186

34 - Cuckoo about Cuckoos 191

35 - There Are No Flies On Us 197

36 - Of Tyrants and Trillions, Part I 202

37 - Of Tyrants and Trillions, Part II 207

Preface

WHEN I WAS a young man I thought that metaphysics was the most exciting (and important) thing in the world. I even had a friend whose ambition it was to place the whole of human knowledge on a different, and of course a much firmer, metaphysical basis. I have lost touch with him, but as far as I am aware he did not succeed. If he did, I have not heard.

I wish now that I had not wasted so much time on the imponderable questions of metaphysics but had used it to more worthwhile effect. Of course, everyone has metaphysical presumptions whether he knows it or not; often these presumptions vary from moment to moment according to need, but I have not noticed that conscious metaphysicians are more consistent or live better than unconscious ones. Rather than study philosophy, I should have studied insects.

In the little essays that follow, I have no grand theory to prove, no single message to convey. Small things and slight occurrences have caught my attention and caused me to reflect a little. I hope only to please the reader. My thanks as ever go to the editor of the *New English Review,* Rebecca Bynum.

1
Apocalypse Now

PRACTICALLY ALL journalism is forgotten the day after it was written, even by those who wrote it. This is fortunate, for it means that the inevitable idiocies of the genre receive a swift and decent burial, never to be disinterred: nothing ever comes back to haunt a journalist and oblivion overcomes all. That is why journalists can afford to be fearlessly outspoken; no one will ever remember, except in the vaguest terms, what they wrote. Fairness, accuracy, consistency: these are qualities with which the journalist can easily, and in some publications must, dispense.

I do not exclude myself from these strictures, far from it. Sometimes at the end of a day when I have written two or even three articles I relax with friends and they ask me what I have written that day. Not only can I not remember the details, I cannot remember even the subject of my articles. Keats thought that his name was writ in water; in what then, we might ask, are journalists' name written? Perhaps they are not written at all.

The evanescence of one's effusions in print notwithstanding, their oneness with Nineveh and Tyre, it is good for the character to reflect upon one's own grosser errors. I was reminded of one of these the other day by a comment posted on the internet about a book I wrote more than a quarter of a century ago, all the more troubling because it was written by someone by no means hostile.

The book was an account of a journey across Africa that I made by such means of public transport as I could find. On that journey I passed through Rwanda—about seven years before a genocide of the kind that was supposed never to happen again after the Second World War. I was of course aware of the conflict between the Hutu and the Tutsi (whom I remember a Belgian expatriate describing as 'the long, tall ones') but I gave as my firm opinion, founded upon only the slightest and most superficial acquaintance with the country, that the conflict had by then been settled once and for all, irredeemably, in favour of Hutu predominance and power. President Juvenal Habyarimana was so firmly in power that it was difficult to believe that he would ever be unseated from it; his National Revolutionary Movement for Development, the only permitted political party, was ubiquitous. Children became members of it, *ex officio*, at the moment of their birth; they had no choice in the matter and there was no escaping it, notwithstanding the fact that one's political opinions at the age of an hour are a little undeveloped.

It seemed to me likewise indisputable that Rwanda was, by African standards, an efficient and well-administered state. You had only to stand at the frontier with Zaire (as the Democratic Republic of the Congo then was) to see that this was so. On the one side, the Congolese, all was disorder and chaos; on the other, the Rwandan, all was order and neatness. This might have been as much to do with the pressure of circumstances as with the political arrangements, for while humans to work the land were in short supply in Zaire, land for humans to work was in short supply in Rwanda. The one circumstance favoured carelessness, the other care; perhaps the respective political regimes of the two countries were irrelevant to the evident difference in the way the land was looked after on either side of the frontier. After all, Mobutu had a sole political party of his own, the Popular Movement of the Revolution, to match Habyarimana's. The difference between Rwanda and Zaire was like that between North Korea and Cuba, and whether one prefers one's dictatorships ferociously obsessional or slovenly bohemian is a matter of taste.

Anyway, I did not foresee the invasion of Tutsi exiles, driven out of the country by previous ethnic violence, only two years later: an invasion that would lead before long to what was possibly the most thorough and efficient attempted genocide in history. Such, then were my powers of prediction, my insight into the workings of the future: I was completely oblivious to the approach of one of the greatest political catastrophes of my adulthood.

I was not alone in this, of course; but not many of those who failed to foresee it committed themselves so firmly to paper. One interesting question that I have never seen asked let alone answered, is whether, had the invading rebels foreseen the genocide that their invasion unleashed, they would have acted any differently? In other words, would they have sacrificed the attainment of power to save the lives, or rather to prevent the murder, of hundreds of thousands of their kinsmen? Either they foresaw the genocide or they didn't; if they didn't they were as blind as I, which is some consolation to me for my lack of powers of foresight.

Lack of knowledge of a country or a situation never stopped anyone from prognosticating about it. In his famous book about the Anschluss of 1938, and the subsequent dismemberment of Czechoslovakia, called *Fallen Bastions*, the then-celebrated British correspondent, G. E. R. Gedye, who wrote for both the *Times* of London and the *New York Times*, tells how he wrote an article soon after his arrival in Vienna in which he praised the charming and easy-going tolerance of the people, published by ill-chance on the very day of a vicious pogrom against the city's Jewish population. And even if Gedye were on closer acquaintance to write no more on the celebrated *Gemütlichkeit* of the Viennese, even if he were to become only too aware of the extreme brutality of the triumphant Nazis (he wrote the book, 500 closely-printed pages long, at high speed in the British legation in Prague, whither he had been expelled by the Gestapo), even he who had read *Mein Kampf* and was aware both of what he called its 'insane incitements against the Jews' and its clear blueprint for a general war which he took completely and correctly at face value, why even he had no inkling of the approaching Holocaust. He foresaw—as he saw—endless persecution of Jews, but he did not foresee their total annihilation.

Even close acquaintance with a situation, then, and study of it to the exclusion of all other objects of the mind, does not guarantee insight into the future, even in rough outline, and even only a few years off. When, for example, I was in Central America during the era of civil wars there, virtually all the foreigners who had made the region the object of their researches believed that the triumph of socialist revolutions was inevitable, in the sense of being immanent in the present and the past. This was in part wishful thinking—I met no one who thought such revolutions both inevitable and bad—but I doubt that many of them have acknowledged their mistake since to the extent of abjuring further prognostications. Like me, they make excuses for their own lack of foresight. And for this I do not entirely blame them, for Man is a prognosticating animal, he peers into the future as a short-sighted man at landscape. But often he makes no clear distinction between what will happen, and what will happen unless something else intervenes. It is a crucial distinction, for that 'something else' is precisely what cannot be predicted.

If only time ran backwards rather than forwards, how much wiser we should be! But time, it seems, makes fools of us all; there surely can be no one who has never confidently predicted what never happened.

One way to avoid humiliation by time is to impose no time limits upon one's predictions. This is the technique of all financial experts. For some years I have received by internet various financial newsletters which mainly catch my attention by predicting an economic apocalypse and giving me only three days to take avoiding action to ensure the value of my paltry investments. The newsletters speak of collapse, meltdown, crisis, even Armageddon. My wealth will be halved, quartered, decimated; I might be left penniless, and at my time of life I will have no time to recover my losses. The depression will last for years, decades; sometimes the newsletters state that in the entire history of the world there has never been a recovery from a financial situation like this, in other words that we are entering the economic dark ages. Gangs of the ruthless desperate will roam the ruined cities, robbing everyone of everything. The last few years of my earthly existence will be lived out in Hobbesian misery amidst the rubble of civilisation.

Quite right, I think! I always knew the world was going to the dogs, and here is the confirmation of it. The graphs provided prove it! Debt of all kinds is increasing exponentially, the balance of trade is unfavourable, the demographics appalling. Soon half the population will be over ninety, and the other half will have to look after them. Abandon hope, all ye who read online here.

No, that is premature. It so happens that the financial newsletters have just the strategy for the enlightened and prudent few such as I (oh, how flattering!) to avoid the catastrophe. It all seems to me a little like those back garden nuclear fallout shelters that they used to try to sell us in the days when nuclear war was more feared than financial collapse—perhaps there is a law of the conservation of anxiety as well as of energy. But just because nuclear war hadn't happened yet never meant that it wasn't about to happen. And I myself have often preached, or at least implied, that social collapse is near. Imminent catastrophe is more interesting to contemplate than dull continuity. Besides, pessimists are seldom disappointed.

But whom can you trust? The week before the Crimean crisis broke, I was strongly advised by one of the financial newsletters to buy Russian shares. I didn't follow the advice, for two reasons, the stronger being inertia and the better being that I trust the Russians to play the game of capitalism fairly and honestly about as much as I would trust a great white shark to eat up its greens. Within a week of the advice the Moscow index was down by twenty per cent or more: that, of course, would have been the time to buy, for I knew that the index would be up again almost immediately once the preening impotence of the Mr Obama and the European Union (here a prediction would have been almost certain) became obvious even to the fund managers.

Just as there is compassion fatigue, so that depictions of terrible suffering no longer excite our desire to alleviate it, so I now suffer from apocalypse fatigue. No firm date is ever given for the supposed forthcoming apocalypse, such that if it fails to happen by that date the theory by which it was predicted stands refuted. Old apocalypses never die, therefore; they just recede into the mental background, while another comes into the foreground. But my financial newsletters have warned me for so long and so often that the end is nigh, that doom is at hand, while all the time I seem to have become somewhat more prosperous by the simple expedient of spending less than I earn and keeping my more luxurious instincts under control, that I no longer take any conscious notice of them. They—the financial newsletters—are like those religious enthusiasts who predict the end of the world on next Thursday afternoon, but seem hardly disconcerted at all when it does not happen, and merely move the date forward by ten days.

They are also like those epidemiologists who predict that the next flu epidemic will be of a mutated virus so virulent that it will wipe out half of humanity. The epidemic duly comes, and half of humanity is not wiped out; the epidemiologists smoothly transfer their hope, if such it may be called, to the next epidemic.

There is a famous passage in *The Problems of Philosophy* by Bertrand Russell, first published in 1912, in which the difficulty of induction is clearly laid out.

> The man who has fed the chicken every day throughout its life at last wrings its neck instead, showing that more refined views as to the uniformity of nature would have been useful to the chicken.

A thousand apocalypses that have not happened do not mean that there will be no apocalypse tomorrow. A large part of wisdom, therefore, is in knowing when things will and will not repeat themselves, and to what extent. There is no formula for it, not even in principle.

2
Destructive Creation

WHEN I WAS a small boy adults used to say to me, 'If you ask a silly question, you'll get a silly answer.' This irritated my nascent sense of logic: for if I genuinely did not know the answer to my question, how could I possibly be expected to know that it was silly? And could anything be silly in the absence of knowledge that it was? This was my childish equivalent of Socrates' or Plato's doctrine that no one does wrong willingly: a doctrine that does not accord with my clinical experience as a doctor, let alone with my experience of life. But at the time, the accusation of silliness seemed to me worse than merely wrong: it was unjust. I did not appreciate at that age that there could be such a thing as a responsibility to know, even if one did not.

One of silliest questions I have ever heard, and heard often, is why some or many countries are poor. This is to get everything exactly the wrong way round, as if Man were born rich and had somehow to achieve poverty. Of course, it is possible for those who were formerly rich to become poor, for example by improvidence or the spoliation of others; but immemorial poverty requires no explanation. It is wealth that needs explaining, mankind not having been born in marble halls with a silver spoon in its mouth.

I once bought a slender volume entitled *Why Bad Dogs?* This set out to explain why some dogs barked incessantly, bit the postman, wouldn't walk to heel and so forth. I am such a dog-lover that I find it difficult to put myself in the place of those who dislike dogs, but still I wondered whether the question asked by the title was the correct one. Dog-lover as I am, I am not the Rousseau of dogs; I do not think that canine nature, untouched by association with humans, is good; and if I were writing the Social Contract for Dogs, I should not begin 'Dogs are born mute, but everywhere they bark.'

Clearly it is important to frame one's questions correctly if one wants a real answer: often one does not, for the interrogative is not always used simply to obtain information but also to confound and irritate, as every child knows. The other day I came across a book published in 1937 by A R Powys, one of the Powys family that produced so many writers, mostly unread today, though some were well-known in their day and John Cowper Powys still has his devotees. His brother, A R Powys (1882–1936), was an architect and preserver of ancient buildings who also wrote essays on architecture, and one of them in the book that I came across, *From the Ground Up*, was titled 'Origins of Bad Architecture.' This is a question that has long troubled me, so much so that my wife says I have become something of a bore on it. Whenever I see an eyesore in otherwise beautiful surroundings, which is often, I remark upon it, whereupon my wife, who agrees that the twentieth century was an urban aesthetic disaster, tells me I should calm down (eyesores make me angry) because what is done is done, and working myself up about it will do the landscape no good and me harm.

But is the origin of bad architecture the right question to ask, as if it were in the nature of architecture to be good unless some disturbing factor intervened? First, however, I cannot forebear from remarking on the frontispiece of the book, a photo of the author. He is a most distinguished-looking man, of a kind that one does not, or at any rate that I do not, see today. If the face is the window of the soul, then this man was aesthetically fastidious, sensitive, inquiring, honest, upright and truthful, a man whom one would feel it peculiarly disgraceful to deceive in even the smallest matters. One cannot imagine him for a moment writing what he did not believe to be true (and therefore he was not a true modern intellectual) or telling a lie. That he was a man of exceptional probity is confirmed in the introduction to the volume written by his most famous brother, John Cowper Powys, admittedly not an entirely unbiased source:

> Nothing in his life was at random. Nothing was wanton or wilful. In dress, in ablution, in food, in drink, in the minutest arrangements of his time, of the objects around him, of his rooms, of his garden, of his household utensils, in lighting a fire, in opening a bottle, in whittling a stick, in driving a nail, in hanging a picture, in washing a dish, in chopping a log, in

> cutting a loaf, he would always follow a carefully considered method of his own, for which when challenged... he would bring forth a most confounding and irrefutable weight of elaborate justification.

Such integrity in everything that he did is perhaps slightly intimidating to us lesser mortals who have it not, but it nevertheless has the enormous merit of not taking anything in life for granted, in paying close attention to every small thing, of finding purpose everywhere, and therefore of avoiding the blight of modern life, namely meaninglessness and boredom. These are much underestimated factors in the promotion of social pathology in our societies, and explain the restless, constant and self-defeating search for entertainment or distraction, or that for all-encompassing ideologies or self-absorbing causes among people of rather more intellectual disposition. The integrity of A R Powys, I say, is inscribed on his face, though here I must add a small caveat: physiognomy is not an exact science, though we all practise it, and when I first saw a picture of Mr Madoff, him of the century and a half prison sentence, I confess that I saw in him just the kind of calm, thoughtful and honest man to whom I should have liked to entrust my money, such as it is.

The integrity of A R Powys notwithstanding, is the question he asks, that of what makes for bad architecture, the right one? Should we not rather be asking, 'What is good architecture?' and then, when we have decided this question, examine in what ways bad architecture habitually departs from the answer we have given?

This Powys specifically denies. Indeed, it is his position that theorising about the principles of good architecture, especially when it is believed that they have been found, is one of the sources of bad architecture. I am not sure he is absolutely right in this: Palladio, Vitruvius and Alberti all theorised about architecture, not without a certain practical success. But they were a long time ago, and the theorists of his time were a lot less trustworthy: they had a deeply destructive impulse or instinct, perhaps strengthened by or even originating in the catastrophe that was the First World War. If that—the war—is what our civilisation wrought, it is time for something completely new and different.

The problem of bad architecture is more acute in Europe than anywhere else in the world, in large part because Europe has such an immemorial tradition of great and, more to the point, good vernacular architecture. The aesthetically bad is much more painful to behold in proximity to the good than it is when everything around it is bad. Then it is like a wound to the eye. That is why, if anyone wants to study bad architecture, he should go to Paris.

A strange choice, you say! Is not Paris the City of Light? Is it not the most beautiful city in the world, with the possible exception of Venice? Quite so: that is why it is so essential to study what has been built there in the second half of the twentieth century, for there is no modern architecture in the world worse than French. Go to the Tour Montparnasse, thou architect, consider its ways and be wise (or to the Centre Pompidou or Musée du Quai Branly, for that matter).

It is true, perhaps, that modern architecture in France has passed its nadir (one certainly hopes so, for no nadir was, if I may be allowed a neologism, nadirer than the French), but even now it cannot rise above a glassy, saurian, impersonal elegance indistinguishable from the same kind of building in Manila or Santiago, and towards which it is, and will always be, impossible to feel any individual affection or warmth. This architecture is for the cold-blooded, for 'communication' rather than for speech.

I have asked architects and architectural historians why it is that we in Europe are incapable of building a single charming house, let alone an entire urban environment that is other than a visual nightmare. The answers they have given are various (none has dared deny the premise of the question).

They say that we cannot use the methods, materials or designs of the past. This seems to me inexact. I can quite see that, for economic and social reasons, it is impossible to use the methods and perhaps the materials of the past. A bricklayer or stonemason now commands too high a wage for his manual labour to make it possible for houses or other buildings to be built on any scale in the old fashion. The bricklayer or mason himself expects to live at a standard of living not so very different from that of the person for whom he is building.

But design, at least in Europe, is another question altogether. There is actually no reason at all why old designs cannot be reproduced, albeit with mass-produced materials. Indeed, in London recently a housing authority did precisely this; it copied precisely the elegant early Victorian buildings (still of Regency inspiration) of three sides of a residential square in restoring the fourth side. It did not use Victorian methods, but it used Victorian designs, with triumphant result, far, far better than any residential architecture of the recent past.

Why was this expedient never thought of before? Why instead was so much ugliness—and ugliness on a new and inhuman scale—constructed not merely *faute de mieux* or as a necessary evil in the unfortunate circumstances, but with the proud ideological rodomontade of the entire architectural profession, a rodomontade in which even now it has not ceased to indulge? (No profession likes to face up to its crimes, of course.)

The reason, I suspect, is not merely economic, for even where no expense is spared the result is usually catastrophic. The reason is much deeper.

Modern man's religion is progress: what comes later must be better than what went before. And there are clearly whole fields of human endeavour in which this is so. No one, I suppose, would wish to be operated upon by surgeons using the methods of 1830. (Even in medicine, however, it is sometimes worth remembering that the very latest is not necessarily the very best, and the supposition that it is has occasionally led to disaster.)

But aesthetics are not science: aesthetics do not show the same inbuilt tendency to improvement. From the aesthetic point of view what comes after is not necessarily better than what went before, and is often worse, even much worse. Particularly in an age of progress, however, men are reluctant to admit that they cannot do better than their forebears; to admit it is to admit the heresy that beauty's arrow, unlike that of time, does not fly in one direction only. A return to the pattern or design of the past—dismissed as *pastiche*, the worst of all architectural crimes, far worse than destroying an immemorial townscape—would indicate a deficiency of imagination, inventiveness and originality, all the qualities that make the *artist*, at least in the romantic conception of the artist. And architects, in their own conception, are above all *artists*: artists, moreover, when it is widely believed that the purpose of art is to challenge, to question, to transgress, never to celebrate, to harmonise, to console, to give meaning.

How different from the spirit of A R Powys, of whom his brother writes:

> The bulk of his life's work lies where he would have had it lie, in the silent and unapplauding masonry and timber of the irreplaceable buildings he saved from ruin...

He draws attention to his 'self-effacement,' a characteristic that architects today—like almost everyone else—rejects as treason to the self.

Le Corbusier, writing of the years pre-dating the First World War, said that there was no architecture of the time, that architecture was dead. He used this as a pretext and justification for his own purely destructive and megalomaniac impulses. But what he said was simply not true, as the most casual inspection of Paris will inform anyone with eyes to see.

Recently I stayed in Paris for three weeks, in an apartment block built in 1905, precisely the time of which Le Corbusier wrote so contemptuously. It was in an arrondissement that was once unfashionable but has since gone up in the world, in no small part thanks to apartment blocks such as the one in which I stayed. My block was elegant and obviously owed something to art nouveau; it was not great architecture in the way that the Parthenon or the Taj Mahal are great architecture, but it was highly civilised, pleasing to the eye, functional and helped to create one of the most agreeable urban environments the world has known. Needless to say, it was in keeping with what already existed around it.

The reward of the architect, now otherwise completely forgotten, was his name, carved in small letters, on stone facing, together with that of the builder: the same as on other, equally elegant and agreeable apartment blocks. He understood, as so many architects today do not seem or want to understand, that egotism is a deadly sin in architects, the deadliest in fact, and that A R Powys' happy mixture of pride and modesty was very necessary. And the pride must be in the work, not the person.

3
What a Falling Prof. Was There

LAST NIGHT I could not sleep: the clocks had gone forward (or back, I always find it difficult to remember which) and I had drunk a bit too much earlier in the evening. I don't know why, but I suddenly had the idea to occupy my sleeplessness by looking up on the internet some of the distinguished doctors I had known as a student and young man. Perhaps this strange impulse came to my mind because recently, in my e-mail, I have received, both from France and from England, invitations to insure myself against funeral costs. Do the advertisers know something about me that I do not know myself? They cannot have got it from my doctor because I never go to my doctor. Perhaps they are working from general principles, namely that people of my age have accelerating death rates after years of declining ones. It is therefore nothing personal. But it is clear that advertisers of whom I have never heard know my date of birth, which is creepy enough by itself. (What else do they know about me?) At any rate, I will soon be going the way of those distinguished doctors I looked up, most of whom were dead; and I was seized by nostalgia.

On the internet one thing leads to another and I ended up looking also for my student contemporaries with whom I had since lost touch. The internet acts on sleep rather as amphetamines do, that is to say it prevents it. I found myself looking for hours.

The first thing I noticed was how misleading an impression in general the internet gave of the relative distinction of my own and the previous generation. The previous generation lived before the internet era so that only scraps of information about it were to be found on it; whereas there were often entire screeds about my contemporaries who seem to do nothing without an electronic record of it appearing. Their lives had become public in a way that those of the preceding generation had never been. And yet I cannot rid my mind of my belief that the previous generation had been composed of worthier men, men of deeper character, more distinguished in their distinction, than our own. We are shallow by comparison with them; spoilt in childhood, we have grown up pygmies. The only compensation for this melancholy thought is that the next generation will be even worse.

I have of course considered the possibility that the reason the previous generation appears to me so much more distinguished than my own is that I know my own generation better; as no man is a hero to his valet, so no generation seems distinguished to those who shared its youth. You can think really highly only of those about whom you know little. I knew the previous generation only by its accomplishments, not by its *bêtises*; with my generation it was the other way round.

I lived as a student in a house in which the physical squalor was equal only to the intellectual ferment. One of my fellow-residents published a paper in *Nature* before he had even graduated, but we thought nothing of this as an accomplishment simply because he was one of us. Of the four who shared the house, three became eminent professors (one published a paper only last week that was widely reported in newspapers). Of the four, only I failed to become a professor, my career, if such it can be called, having followed an erratic and one might say unserious path. The then girlfriend of one of us became a world expert on an important if declining disease, and many of our friends and associates likewise became professors of some eminence.

Even so, I cannot, as I said, entirely rid myself of the feeling that we amounted to nothing much. The fact that the title of professor, once awarded so sparingly, seems nowadays to be given out like titles of nobility in times when monarchical governments needed to raise money by the sale of such titles, reinforces my belief. It is precisely our generation, after all, that has cheapened that of professor by inflating the numbers of professors along with debt. This title was given so sparingly before our generation's arrival to maturity that it was a virtual guarantee of genuine distinction in the person upon whom it had been conferred. It is not that there are no professors of distinction left, rather that there are so many without.

I looked up one man with whom I had worked as a young doctor. He was a year or two older than I, and he has been a professor at a university reputed to be one of the best twenty or so in the world for many years. When I first knew him, he and I were at an age when a year or two's advancement in the hierarchy still seemed considerable, representing a great advance in experience. But I spotted him then for a charlatan, and a charlatan he has remained, at least if a video of him posted on the internet is anything to go by.

He dressed himself with more care than a reigning monarch, his chief concern being to mark himself out from others (not, when you come to think of it, indicative of a very flattering opinion of others). If I remember aright he was much in favour of velvet and corduroy, with unusually-coloured shoes. He wore silk around his neck, semi-cravat and semi-scarf. All his accoutrements, from his pen to his attaché case, were unusual and such as no one else had. He smoked big cigars, which was unusual, not to say unique, at his age and in that *milieu*, which was medical. I think he wanted to give off the aura of Freud without actually being a Freudian.

His genius, if such it can be called, was in discovering the possibilities of going interdisciplinary. He realised that going interdisciplinary would always give him an escape route: among the *a*'s he could always claim be a *b*, and among the *b*'s he could always claim to be an *a*, which would explain why no one could ever quite understand what he was saying. Everyone would blame himself rather than him for not being able to understand what on earth he was going on about; every a would assume it was because he knew nothing of *b*-ology, while every b would assume it was because he knew nothing of *a*-ology. It was a perfect tactic at a time of university expansion.

I cannot of course say that he employed it consciously, and personally I rather liked him. But I did not notice much irony about him, or even a deep sense of humour. He once invited me to dinner (he lived in a charmingly bohemian flat, full of ethnoiserie) and he was a generous host and charming dinner companion. After a very good dinner—cooked by his wife of course—he suggested that we listen to some music. He asked me to choose, bearing in mind that he knew nothing later than the Twelfth Century. My knowledge of pre-Twelfth Century music, I am afraid, has since remained as exiguous as it was then, but I admired, in a way, the manner in which he announced the nature of his collection, as if it were the most natural thing in the world to a man of discrimination.

In those days I had every confidence that his charlatanry would find him out, that the fact that he was so transparently acting a part would prevent him from getting on in the world, let alone have a very successful career, much more successful than my own. But he had realised, as I had not, that the world was changing; and that, in the matter of academic advancement, solid merit was not the easiest or best way to get on. The academic world, or that part of it with the power to appoint staff, had become as enthralled (or perhaps I should say enthralable) by charlatanry as some of the American population is by transparently crooked and bogus television evangelists. I did not understand that the key text to understanding the new world that was then in the process of birth was Hans Christian Andersen's *The Emperor's New Clothes*. No doubt this little story is of some application in all times and all places (it is truly universal, at least of man in a state of civilisation) but never had it been so applicable to academic life. My young acquaintance—I cannot call him a friend—fell into a university chair like a ripe apple falls to the ground.

I watched him (on You Tube) give a lecture and laughed heartily. He was not so much serious as earnest. This is a prime distinction which in the modern world is seldom made. There was no hint in his manner of the successful rogue. He was very professorial in manner, to the extent of having a very slight speech impediment of the type that English intellectuals, especially left-wing ones, often have (but proletarians never do). His manner of dress had changed from vaguely Tennysonian to young server in a hip and expensive bar. His hair, which had always been intellectually curly, had now gone white: but he still wore his Isaac Deutscher-type beard. Such a beard, I think he supposed, lent weight to his words, and possibly, from the point of view of others, it did. A *bon viveur*, he had put on weight.

He had not been found out and had gone through life in a pleasant and not unlucrative manner, lucubrating incomprehensibly and yet always with a vague penumbra of meaning. I do not mean to deprecate this: it is a definite skill that I personally have not mastered. Try as I might sometimes to be incomprehensible, and therefore profound, meaning keeps peeping through what I say like the sun through clouds. I suppose it is a matter of willpower and practice. I have never really wanted enough to be incomprehensible; and I am far too literal-minded for my language not to alight before long upon concrete realities.

I do not envy my former acquaintance his academic success; I would not wish to have spent my life with his thoughts running through my head because they would have bored me terribly. In other words, I cannot really imagine what it would have been like to be him, for I assume that he was never bored with himself or by his misty thoughts. Like everyone else, though, he has added to the rich tapestry of life:

none of us can do otherwise.

Still, I cannot help but compare him with, say, a professor whom I knew as a student of whom no one had an unkind word to say. He died twenty years ago (as I discovered during my sleepless night's surfing of the internet), and if he had not he would now be almost a hundred. He had the perfect manners of a previous, more courtly age; he was soft-spoken and induced obedience in his juniors by natural authority and because no one would have wished to upset him. In short he was a gentleman. He had written the most important textbook on a disease that has since only gained in public health importance. It is in the nature of things that the most learned textbooks on scientific subjects, though they may take years to write, should be superseded within ever-decreasing periods; indeed, the very notion of a textbook is now superseded; and thus to write one was a work of abnegation where it was not one of naked ambition (which it certainly was not in this man's case). It was a service to mankind and intended as such.

When he retired, he concentrated on gardening (do really wicked men ever garden?). He wrote a book about an aspect of that delicate, useful and popular art that is acknowledged to be the best available in its field. Then he died, beloved of all.

Old men don't forget, or at any rate when they don't they compare. When I compare the two professors I think, with apologies to Hamlet senior:

> … what a falling off was there!
> From him, whose love was of that dignity
> That it went hand in hand even with the vow
> He made to knowledge, and to decline
> Upon a wretch whose natural gifts were poor
> To those of his.

No doubt it is foolish, even dangerous, to found a whole theory of cultural decline upon a comparison of two people, chosen perhaps to prove the pre-determined theory. And yet, and yet…

4
A Game of Rat and Mouse

RATS I ABOMINATE, but mice—wild mice, that is, including house mice, not the white laboratory kind with pink eyes—I have always sympathised with and had much time for. They seem always to be, if I may so put it, underdogs: in a perpetual state of fear, no doubt justified. When I see one quivering in a corner I wish to protect it rather than add to the already considerable number of its enemies—cats, owls, hawks, weasels, snakes and so forth. My wife, far from climbing onto a chair and screaming, feels the same; and I think of a line from Christopher Smart, the mad Kit Smart with whom Dr Johnson would 'as lief prayed as with anyone else,' about the mouse in his poem *Jubilate Agno* (*Rejoice in the Lamb*):

> For the mouse is a creature of most excellent valour...

Is that not correct? A tiger needs no bravery, except perhaps in tackling another tiger, but a mouse takes its life in its paws every time it leaves its nest. They are not brave who know no fear, but those who fear and yet venture forth. The poem continues most movingly:

> For this is a true case -
> Cat takes female mouse,
> Male mouse will not depart,
> but stands threat'ning and daring.
> If you will let her go,
> I will engage you,
> As prodigious a creature as you are.

For the Mouse is a creature
Of great personal valour.
For the Mouse is of
An hospitable disposition.

No doubt strict biologists would deride these lines as absurdly anthropomorphic, but strict biologists have far greater difficulty in escaping from anthropomorphism and the language of intention than they usually acknowledge. The strictest Darwinists often speak as if Evolution were a person and instil it (or Him) with a purpose as well as a process. They would, perhaps, explain this lapse as being caused by a biologically-predetermined tendency for sapient beings to imbue the world, and therefore descriptions of the world, with intentionality, which it is the duty of scientific puritans to try to eliminate. I do not enter the argument as to whether they are right to want to do so, but only remark that people like Kit Smart, who express some affective kinship with mice, are likely to prove nicer people, and more amusing company, than those who see mice as automata.

Of course I acknowledge that my affection for mice is largely based upon ignorant sentimentality. I never trapped them or even tried to poison them when, as a student, there were many of them in my house. (Now that I have accumulated a considerable library with a number of rare books, I have for the first time resorted to rat and mouse poison, for mice are, if not avid readers exactly, avid consumers of books. Did not Karl Marx himself say in his preface to *A Contribution to a Critique of Political Economy* that he and Engels left the manuscript of *The German Ideology* to the gnawing criticism of the mice? But even so, I should not have laid the poison had I not been assured that its effect was to make the mice leave the house and die—of internal bleeding, actually—outside in the garden. This was typical bourgeois sentimentality, I am sure that some critics will say: he does not want to see mice agonising in front of him, or be confronted by the smell of their decomposing bodies consequent upon his actions. For him, it is a matter of out of sight, out of mind, just as, when he invests his money in some company or other, he knows and cares nothing about its treatment of its workers, its polluting activities, and so forth. Thus he waxes sentimental about a mouse in a corner, with its bright little eyes and quivering whiskers, but poisons them wholesale in his library. Typical! How much better and more honest it would be if he did his own dirty work and set traps, dealing with the dead or dying mice himself rather than leaving it to Nature to do his dirty work for him out in the garden.)

I have also long been aware of the role of mice in spreading illness such as leptospirosis or Weill's disease, also known as rat-catcher's disease. But even when as a student I lived in close proximity to many mice, as measured by the number of their droppings, I resolved to do nothing about them, preferring rather to await the development of an illness and then treat it as leptospirosis (the principal danger of the disease lying in delayed diagnosis) rather than eliminate the mice wholesale.

My attitude to rats is very different, I need hardly say. I feel no pity for them. The rat I regard as malign and wicked who does harm for the sheer pleasure of doing it. He is intelligent enough to know better. He is sneaky—he is not called a rat for nothing—and spends his day planning his depredations and his conquest of the world. Rats will survive long after Man destroys himself. Whenever I see a rat, which is not often considering that, according to those who have studied them, you are never further than a few yards from one, I have no compunction in chasing him with a spade, which I would bring down upon him with the full force at my disposal if I caught up with him, which somehow I never do. In the back of my mind I am always concerned not to corner him, for a cornered rat jumps and goes straight for your throat, at least he does in my imagination. There is nothing to be said for the rat; for the rat is a creature of most determined evil.

Now voles are more like mice than rats, at least I think they are. They are delightful creatures to look at and seem harmless. One of the most interesting books I have ever read is Charles Elton's magisterial *Voles, Mice and Lemmings: Problems in Population Dynamics*. It was handsomely produced in 1942 by the Oxford University Press, and one is full of admiration that such scholarly work (admittedly the summary of many years' study) should have continued in the midst of the great historical cataclysm. It is written in far more leisurely style than would be permitted today and describes the field vole, often called the field mouse. Here is the description of the vole:

> [He] wears a livery entirely suitable to his surroundings: his coat is a short jacket of russet over a dull brown waistcoat; his clothing is completed by white small-clothes, altogether a fine costume for a life in the fields. He makes up for any poverty in his surroundings by an unquenchable activity. He takes no notice of the sun but works morning, noon, and night. With such incessant activity, and taste for almost every

> kind of crop, it is not surprising that the vole makes a success of life.

It is not difficult, I think, to detect a tone of affection and even admiration in this; I suppose a strict evolutionist would say that of course the vole wears a livery entirely suitable to his surroundings, for if he did not he would not be in his, but in some other, surroundings: or alternatively go extinct. His livery is suitable to his surroundings and he lives in his surroundings because his livery is suitable to them.

In fact the vole in Europe has long been an enemy of Man, for every few years his numbers increase explosively and destroy the crops for miles around:

> It is an impressive picture of insurgent subterranean activity, of devastation breaking like a flood upon the crops. All man's vigilance and care are taxed by the multitude of small, swift, flitting forms that infest the ground and devour all living plants. Poison, ploughing, fumigation, trenches, and prayers, all these can scarcely stop the destruction. Gérard [the author of a book about the fauna of his native region, Alsace] remembered an outbreak that happened in 1822, when he was a boy. In that year Alsace was absolutely in the power of mice. 'It was a living and hideous scourging of the earth, which appeared perforated all over, like a sieve.'

Astonishingly to me, the author says of Aristotle's 'measured and balanced description of the rise and fall of a mouse [vole] population might be taken for a text of the present book'—a book, incidentally of immense length. Aristotle, in the *Historia Animalium*, wrote:

> The rate of propagation of field mice in country places, and the destruction they cause, are beyond all telling. In many places their number is so incalculable that but very little of corn-crop is left to the farmer; and so rapid is their mode of proceeding that sometimes a small farmer will one day observe that it is time for reaping, and on the following morning, when he takes his reapers afield, he finds his entire crop destroyed. Their disappearance is unaccountable: in a few days not a mouse will be there to be seen.

According to Elton, a plague of voles struck Germany in 1917 and 1918, making food even scarcer, and thereby lessening Germany's will and ability to continue the war. The voles it was that stabbed Germany in the back.

The sudden decline of vole populations that had equally suddenly exploded made the estimation of the efficacy of efforts to control vole plagues very difficult. Elton tells us:

> Voles multiply. Destruction reigns. There is dismay, followed by outcry, and demands to Authority. Authority remembers its experts, or appoints some: they ought to know. The experts advise a Cure. The Cure can be almost anything: golden mice, holy water from Mecca, a Government Commission. A culture of bacteria, poison, prayers denunciatory or tactful, a new god, a trap, a Pied Piper. The Cures have only one thing in common: with a little patience they always work. They have never been known entirely to fail. Likewise they have never been known to prevent the next outbreak.

Here in essence is the problem that bedevils so much of our thinking: the grandiose assumption that because x was done before y happened, y happened because x was done. It has taken medical practitioners two millennia to free itself from this illusion.

Until I read Elton, I had assumed that H G Wells (whose genius is insufficiently appreciated) had invented, or foreseen, the idea of bacteriological warfare in his story *The Stolen Bacillus*, written in 1894. But it is possible that he was inspired by the experiments conducted in France by Jean Danysz, who in 1892 and 1893 tried to spread mouse typhoid among voles to control their numbers (Danysz himself had discovered the causative germ). The results were equivocal, partly because the experiments were insufficiently controlled and partly because Danysz sowed so much of his bait in the fields—bread soaked in culture of the germ—that it was uncertain whether an epidemic had been started among the voles, or they had simply each eaten of the bait individually and died of it in effect as of a poison. Danysz was also criticised because it was possible—indeed, so it eventually turned out—that the germ was potentially dangerous to man. To prove that it wasn't, Danysz swallowed a whole beaker-full, repeating Pettenkofer's famous attempted refutation of Koch's discovery that the *cholera vibrio* was the cause of cholera. Both Pettenkofer and Danysz forgot that a necessary cause was not the same as a sufficient cause. Is there any of us who has never made the same mistake?

Charles Elton's wonderful book, nearly 500 large and closely-printed pages long, remains, I suppose, largely undisturbed upon the shelves, where it is destined to remain until 'de-accessioned,' to use the euphemism of librarians more destructive of libraries than mere mice for the chucking out of books. At the end of his book, Elton makes an impassioned plea that the population dynamics of mice, voles and lemmings be understood 'not for power alone, but on account of… the beauty of the unstable fabric of the living cosmos.'

To which we can only murmur both 'Amen' and 'Fat chance!'

5
Hitching to Gomorrah

WHEN I WAS sixteen years of age my parents allowed me to hitch-hike my way round England, Scotland, Ireland, France and Switzerland. Perhaps they were pleased to disembarrass themselves of a youth who, around them at least, was sullen and uncommunicative; but what would nowadays seem a decision of parental irresponsibility did not then seem at all extraordinary. I doubt that many parents now would give their sixteen year-old son such permission; but I am not sure whether this tells us more about the increased dangerousness of the world or a change in parental attitudes towards risk.

Certainly it seemed a gentler, and therefore a freer, world in certain respects. Sometimes I would hitch-hike on my own, sometimes with a French friend. I remember once arriving together in the northern industrial city of Leeds late one rainy day; the youth hostel was closed for the night and hotels were beyond our means. We went to a police station and a friendly desk-sergeant, seeing that we were naïve but well-behaved adolescents, put us in a cell overnight on his own authority, that is to say without any reference to the rules that almost certainly would prevent him nowadays from acting in this way. The following morning, at an early hour unfamiliar to most of the middle classes, a policeman woke us from our bed of concrete and gave us a cup of tea before sending us on our way. We thought the world was a friendly place.

In the countryside we practised what the French call '*camping sauvage*,' wild camping, without fear or interference: that is to say we pitched our tents whenever we were tired and wherever we could find what seemed to us a good enough corner. In Europe, at least, such camping is now strictly forbidden, *verboten, vietato, prohibido*, the inevitable consequence, I suppose, of the vast increase in the numbers of people moving around. People who wish to camp are now dragooned into camping sites, where there are all kinds of facilities for them. It is one of the ironies of the world that the freer people are to roam, the less worthwhile it is to do so, and the more constrained by regulations their supposed freedom is.

Not that our *camping sauvage* was comfortable, far from it. I can still feel, in my mind's back, the stones poking through the bottom of the tent preventing sleep until sheer tiredness overcame discomfort. And in those days tents were not the hi-tech contraptions they are now, easy to erect and with all *mod. cons.*, homes from home; they were small, cramped and crude canvas affairs, that let the rain through if you so much as touched the inner side of the canvas—which, of course, it was almost impossible not to do, so that one woke in the morning damp and cold. Although I have never been one much for physical discomfort for its own sake, I think that I understood that some of the value of the experience was actually to put up with it; and certainly there were few more ecstatic days of my life than rising early after a bad night's sleep to spend much of the ensuing day eating the wild raspberries that grew on hedges that lined the narrow country roads of Scotland. I have always loved raspberries; but none were ever half so delicious as those.

Once we hitch-hiked round the whole coast of Ireland, from Dublin back to Dublin. In a wild part of Galway we found a soft field, very comfortable for camping, but it was next to a house, to which it evidently belonged and we felt obliged to ask permission of the owner to pitch our tent in it. He was the local doctor, and by that time in the evening was perfectly drunk, his bottle of whiskey on the table beside his armchair.

> 'Tell your friend,' he said (for these were the days of President De Gaulle), 'that I think De Gaulle's a f.....g bastard.'

This was beyond my French; I translated it as '*M. le Docteur* does not like De Gaulle.' But even if I had been able to translate it more in keeping with its original spirit, I doubt that I would have done so. Strange to relate, even at that late stage in the decomposition of civilisation, I felt girlishly inhibited about the use of bad language. In fact, I still do.

In France, some monks put us up in a monastery. Little did I realise that I was witnessing almost the last generation of people who chose this immemorial way of life; and contrary to my expectation (for at the time I was a militant atheist) I was much impressed by it. The monks were not at all unworldly in their manner, nor were they wretched or dour; they predisposed me greatly in favour of the religious, and later in my life, in Africa, I came to respect and like them ever more, both nuns and monks. Once, when I subsequently wrote an article expressing my admiration for them (though I still had no religious faith), I was astonished by the tone of vituperation and hatred of the responses. It was as if the religious were a deep existential threat to those who responded. For myself, I can only regret that there are no more monks and nuns, and that Africa must now send missionaries to Europe.

One event, which I have recounted before but which was so important to my development that I do not hesitate to recount again (a sign of age, no doubt), occurred when I was hitch-hiking in Scotland. It is astonishing that even in a land as heavily populated as Great Britain there should be areas of wilderness such as the west of Scotland, where inhabitants are very few, you can go do miles without seeing a house, and the roads are one track with passing places at intervals.

It was on one of these roads that a honeymooning couple picked me up. They were an educated couple, teachers if I remember. They exuded an ordinary happiness, that of good people content with their place and duty in the world, that I now find moving. As we were driving, me in the back of the car, we passed a sheep that had evidently been hit by a car, by the side of the road, its green guts spilt from its burst-open abdomen and its legs kicking in what I suppose must have been agony.

The newly-wed wife cried out when she saw it, and in distress said that the sheep was still alive and suffering. Her husband, solicitous that she should not suffer distress herself, said that the sheep had clearly been dead. Then he turned to me and asked me for confirmation that it was dead.

The words 'No, it was still alive,' rose – or descended - to my throat, but I managed to stop myself in time and said instead, 'Yes, it was obviously dead.' 'You see,' said the husband, and the wife, perhaps because she so much wanted to believe what we said, was much relieved.

In that moment, I realised the absurdity of the supposed categorical imperative to tell the truth on all occasions, as Kant would have us believe, irrespective of circumstances. There are situations in which there are higher values than truth, or at least than truth-telling, as every doctor has eventually to learn.

I was also soon proud that the husband, so much older than I (which is to say at least ten years, an eternity when one is sixteen), had enough confidence in my intelligence, understanding and *savoir faire* after his brief acquaintance with me to have entrusted me with his question, that he would surely not had he thought I was of slower apprehension.

Now I often think of that couple, who seemed so happy then, so freshly, hopefully and insouciantly started out on the path to old age that they must now have nearly completed, being already well on into their seventies. How mature and sophisticated they seemed to me at the time, how young and inexperienced they seem to me now in my memory! I hope that their life has been a happy and contented one, as it seemed then to presage, that their children brought them joy and not pain, that no tragedy befell them. In my heart, however, I can hardly believe that it was so, for few of us entirely escape tragedy even if the fleetingness of human existence from the vantage of age were not itself a tragedy. They must long ago have reached the age at which contemplation of the past was more interesting to them than that of the future (as it always has been to me). I thought of them again when I happened on upon the following lines by Edward Fairfax that I had never previously read, and that reflect on that perennial theme of English (and other) poetry, the shortness of life:

> So in the passing of a day doth pass
> The bud and blossom of the life of man,
> Nor e'er doth flourish more, but, like the grass
> Cut down, becometh wither'd pale and wan.
> O! gather then the rose while time thou hast;
> Short is the day, done when it scant began,
>   Gather the rose of love, while yet you may'st
>   Loving be lov'd, embracing be embrac'd.

This, apparently, is very similar, almost a plagiarism, from Spenser: but (in my opinion) improves upon it. Be that as it may, the lines were my madeleine that brought back to life that couple in the lanes of Scotland nearly half a century ago.

Ever since my youth, and in moral recompense for all those people who took me when I was by the side of the road, I have always taken hitch-hikers unless they positively had the appearance of serial killers, which few of them have. I have never had any cause to regret it, and it seems to me a small and very easy way to be generous, to give away something for nothing, and to give hikers a more favourable impression of their fellow-beings and of life in general. One of the ways to destroy trust, an invaluable social asset, is to mistrust when there is no need of it; and mistrust is the most frequent reason given for people not to pick up hitch-hikers. I much regret that there are so few of them nowadays, either because the trust no longer exists to sustain hitch-hiking as a means of getting around (the mistrust of those who give the rides as great as that of those who want them), or because young people now have cars or money enough easily to afford public transport, and render hitch-hiking unnecessary. I regret the latter almost as much as the former, for youth should be an age of exigent means rather than of ease, comfort and opulence.

The other day I picked up a couple, a young Frenchman and a young American woman, who were together, though he spoke little English and she no French. I joked that they had chosen the best method of language tuition, and they laughed.

He was a history student, and his long brown hair was done into dreadlocks, as if he were a Rastafarian. I suppose he must have admired Jamaican culture, since imitation is the highest form of flattery; I did not much approve his choice of cultural model. But he was very polite (I have found even the drunk hitch-hikers polite in France) and I liked him.

When I picked the couple up, I was playing Brahms' marvellous string sextet on my CD player, a work I love. I asked the young man Aimez-vous Brahms? – a question not only about the composer, but an ironic (as I supposed) reference to the title of a famous novel by Françoise Sagan.

He neither caught the literary reference nor did he know anything of Brahms. 'I don't know much about him,' he said. In fact, I am not sure that he had ever heard of him.

I was deeply discomfited, though I did and said nothing to show it. It is, after all, my generation's fault if decent and intelligent young European men (and I was sure that he was a decent and intelligent young man) identify more with Jamaican culture than with European.

The couple were on their way to a festival of Jamaican music. The question now, then, is not Aimez-vous Brahms? but Aimez-vous reggae? A civilization collapses, I thought; but that is just what my elders said. And the young couple were, after all, very nice. Perhaps our civilization will go quietly, nicely.

6
Eternal Youth, Eternal Kitsch

A KIND FRIEND of mine, knowing my interest in such matters, recently sent me a little book containing a collection of inscriptions found in second-hand books collected by a diligent anthologist, a man called H. B. Gooderham. The books were not, on the whole, precious old volumes but rather cheap and relatively recent paperback editions, many of them in rather scruffy condition. Nor were the inscribers famous persons, nor even identifiable. They were, rather, Everyman.

In his brief introduction to the book, the anthologist says that:

> ... the overriding emotion evoked by these inscriptions is one of pathos. At their most basic level all are records of human connections – or at least attempts at human connections – given added poignancy by the fact that all have been discovered among the shelves of second-hand book shops and, for whatever reason, are no longer in the hands of the original dedicatees.

I am wholly in agreement with this: there is nothing quite like an inscription in a book no longer owned by the dedicatee to capture the melancholy, the bittersweetness, of the passage of time, to recall us to our own mortality and to remind us of the vanity of so much of what preoccupies us.

I love looking at the inscriptions in my books, for they are also a powerful stimulant of my imagination. Of course they raise questions that now cannot be answered, but it would be a dull world in which every question could be answered. For example, I have an edition of Julius

Caesar which was published after the MGM film version of 1953, in which Marlon Brando played Mark Antony, James Mason Brutus, John Gielgud Cassius, Deborah Kerr Portia and Greer Garson Calpurnia. It was published with schoolchildren in mind, and the preface says something that I doubt would be permissible in a schoolbook nowadays:

> On the stage and screen Shakespeare's influence is as profound today as when he lived: profound because in this world of joy and sorrow man disobeys Divine Law. Shakespeare the teacher shows us in his 14 tragedies how, when the PRIDE of Coriolanus, the Jealousy of Othello, the REVENGE of Hamlet, the GREED and WEAKNESS of Macbeth, the LUST of Antony, the short-sighted IDEALISM of Brutus, etc., are allowed to dominate man, unhappiness, unrest, and often war result.

Sir John Gielgud, the great actor, provided an introduction to the play, though I am not sure how keen personally he was on the Divine Law, in which he describes actors' difficulty with the play, especially when performed in Roman dress:

> The classical costumes, though becoming and graceful to players of fine physique, can be ridiculous and hampering to men who are too short, too tall, too thin or too fat. There is always the danger of the effect of a lot of gentlemen sitting on marble benches in a Turkish bath.

That is an image that I shall treasure for ever.

The inscription in the front of the book was in a cultivated hand of the kind that I wish I had, but that it is too late in life for me now to learn (in other words, I don't want it enough). The inscription was dated 21 February, 1957 and was signed John. I entertained a brief hope that the John in question might be Gielgud himself, but after a brief search on the internet I found a specimen of Gielgud's handwriting, and it bore no resemblance to that in this book. I will never know who John is—or was, most likely he is no longer with us.

The inscription was as follows:

> To Ted – wishing you great success and realisation of your ambition.

I know who Ted most likely was, or is, for the page is embossed by a stamp: Library of Edward C. Raeburn. Nothing came up on an internet search for that name, and it seems to me likely that it must be at the least 70 years since his birth, probably more, for no one would have given the book to a boy less than 13 years old. John's hand is that of an adult, and in the England of 1957 (and John was English, since he spelled realisation with an s rather than a z), mature men did not address themselves to young people by their first names. I suspect, then, that Edward C Raeburn was born considerably more than 70 years ago.

What was his ambition, and did he realise it? Was it connected to the theatre or films? Did he want to be an actor or director? Surely no one would give the script of the film version of Julius Caesar to someone who wanted to be an electrician or an airline pilot? If Edward C Raeburn wanted to be something in the theatre it is most likely that he failed, except possibly at the lowest level, or else he would be findable on the internet; and most people, after all, do fail in their ambition if they have one at all.

Is failure in ambition failure in life? Is success in ambition success in life? I love failures: and to me a failed actor, one who spends much of his career out of work and is impoverished, is a much more attractive figure, and possibly a more interesting one, than an actor who achieves stardom. Success by his own lights is apt to make a person pleased with himself and therefore not an interesting interlocutor. The man who knows he has not achieved as much as he ought is a better companion.

But to return to my little book sent me by my kind friend: one of the lessons it teaches is that one should never inscribe a book intended as a gift with a poem of one's own, for it is sure to be bad and probably pretentious, ridiculous in the eyes of anyone other than the person one wishes to impress with it. Bad poetry fulfils a social function, of course, for reading bad poetry is an easy way to learn to appreciate good poetry; but still the rule holds that if you feel a compulsion to inscribe a gift with poetry, it is best to quote someone else's.

Declarations of love found in books are particularly poignant, especially when they were written comparatively recently. Here is one written less than five years after the book was published:

> To my darling Husband – We have now been married for 6 very special months. Enjoy memories of our wonderful honeymoon as you read this.

The book in which this was inscribed was *Death on the Nile*, by Agatha Christie, not perhaps the most auspicious of choices of book for such an inscription, since the story is of murder on honeymoon.

Why did this book appear for sale only a few years after the inscription was written? I hardly dare think that life had imitated art. Perhaps the wife of the darling husband had died tragically of natural causes, and he had found this reminder of her too painful to bear: but I doubt it. He surely would have kept the book in those circumstances. Perhaps he rather than she had died and the wife found memories of him too much to bear, but again I rather doubt it. Much more likely, because more commonplace, is that the marriage failed and the couple separated in acrimony, the darling husband being only too eager to dispose of reminders of his mistake (his new girlfriend wouldn't have liked reminders of his previous liaison).

Actually, there was a graphological clue to the instability of the marriage. Graphology is not, any more than is physiognomy, an exact science, but one feature of female handwriting that I have found a useful if not invariable sign of emotional instability is an i dotted with a circle. The hand of people who do this is generally rounded and childish. I have a clear picture of young women who dot their i's with little circles. They are pretty in a rather common way, their hair tends to be blonde, naturally or not, and they wear a lot of mascara and other cosmetics round their eyes, and in general they do not have a light hand with their makeup. They are friendly and jolly, inclined to exhibitionism, but their emotions are shallow if intense. I imagined Anita, the signatory of the inscription, who signed her name with a little circle above its i, as such a one.

The saddest of the inscriptions was written in a more cultivated hand, 'To my dearest Sonia,' on the flyleaf of an edition of *The Arabian Nights* that dated from 1997.

> We've had our own 1000 and 1 nights of marriage – more or less. Three years already! I still discover things about you I love each day or rediscover: your constancy, your generosity, your sense of justice. I count myself a happy man to have found you, and I hope it lasts as many years as we can count.
> I love you. Tom

Who, reading this, can remain unmoved by the sadness its discarding suggests? A human tragedy is implied in a few words, even if we can never know what exactly it was.

One inscription was of sociological moment. It was in a book with the ominously slushy title of *Forever*:

> Dear Claire,
>
> This has got to be a teenage classic! So to a 40 year old from another heres [sic] to forever being a teen.
>
> much love
>
> Nat
> Xxx

Ominously again, the signature was decorated with a little heart, pathognomonic (as we doctors say of a sign that invariably points to a particular illness) of emotional kitsch.

What was most interesting in this, I thought, was the idea that being forever a teenager is something that would be desirable. We all regret our youth as we grow older, and increasingly live in the past, but that is not quite the same as actually wanting to return to adolescence. When I think of my past, it is more with regret than with longing, that I did not use my opportunities better, that I made choices that even at the time I knew to be wrong. If youth knew, if age could, is the old French expression, and it is right.

The Peter-Pan-ism expressed in this inscription is something new. I would have said that somebody might make a fortune if he could produce the elixir of eternal adolescence, except that it is not necessary, for our culture does it for us. It keeps us immature. First comes precocity, then arrested development.

The figure of the ageing rock star is interesting though not inspiring. When one sees pictures of these seventy year-old adolescents one is torn between repulsion and pity. Their faces are canyoned by age and, but with their uncompromisingly youthful hairstyles, dress and comportment, they look like revenants in a budget horror film, as if they have just brushed the clay of the churchyard in which they were buried from their face and body. There are more and more people in our streets who look like this but who have never been rock stars; we grow older as a population, but not with acceptance, let alone grace.

Adolescence, it need hardly be said, is an age of bad taste, when all that is garish and meretricious attracts, and all that is subtle and meritorious repels. To make of adolescence the state in which one wishes to remain is to wish upon the world the permanent triumph of the kitsch, the shallow and the gimcrack. And accordingly, the adolescent sensibility is one that prevails in much of the art world, where the most adolescent of goals, transgression, is still aimed at. Shock the parents, *épater le bourgeois*, such is the golden rule.

The problem is that the parents have long since refused to grow up and the bourgeoisie has long since decamped to Bohemia. It is hardly surprising that so much artistic production now has all the freshness of last week's bread, for few are so conformist as rebellious youth.

7
What Dreams May Come

A FEW NIGHTS AGO, I had an unpleasant dream. Normally I don't remember my dreams and if this one was anything to go by, it is just as well. Dreams may be the royal road to the unconscious, as Freud said they were, but if so it is a road that I don't want to go down. I am insufficiently curious about myself, the world containing so much subject matter of far greater interest to me and others. If the truth be known, I have never been much impressed by psychoanalytic dream interpretation, or psychoanalytic anything else, which seems to me a latter-day form of haruspicy, divination by entrails. We may be such stuff as dreams are made on, but I cannot really believe that dreams are such stuff as we are made on.

Oddly enough I woke from this dream philosophising. The dream was as follows. It was a pitch-black night and I was in the driving seat of my father's car. In my father's day it was an above average car in design and comfort, even mildly luxurious, but when nowadays (as happens very rarely) I see an example of the same, now vintage model creaking down the road, I realise that even the cheapest and smallest of modern vehicles is infinitely its superior in comfort and convenience. Moral progress in the intervening years there may or may not have been, but progress in engineering there most definitely has.

I digress from my dream, a fact which no doubt would seem significant to a psychoanalyst. I had not yet started the car's engine, and decided that I wanted some air. I wound down the window a little, and as soon as it was sufficiently open I felt a hand grab me by the collar in an obviously menacing way. I experienced a moment of panic: should I start the engine first, lock the door or wind up the window? I decided on the latter course, and caught by assailant's fingers in the wound up window. I then fumbled frantically for the keys to start the engine, with the intention of dragging the man (whoever it was) by his fingers along the road, as he so richly deserved. Luckily I woke up before I could start the car and drag him even a few yards.

No doubt there was much possible symbolism in the dream. When I woke, however, I found I was debating in my mind the ethical limits to punishment. That the man who assailed me deserved what I was about to give him I had little doubt, but was that the end of the matter? Assailants must take their chances, but their chances of what, exactly? Being dragged along the road by their fingers caught in a car window?

My scepticism about the interpretation of dreams notwithstanding, what surprised me about this dream was the evident strength and depth of my vengefulness, as if some primitive part of my brain had been activated. I was determined not merely to get away unharmed from my attacker, whoever he was, but to exact revenge upon him. It was not enough that I should evade suffering at his hands; it was necessary that he should now suffer at mine. I was actually going to enjoy inflicting pain on him.

Revenge, as Lord Bacon tells is, is a kind of wild justice; and the desire for it has had a very poor press over the millennia. We are enjoined not to take it, in fact to turn the other cheek to those who strike us, to return good for evil. This is easier said than done: and the question is whether it should be done. Is total forgiveness, that is to say forgiveness in all circumstances, desirable?

What is certainly true is that it is easier to forgive the evil done to others than to forgive the evil done to oneself, especially if in the first place we don't really like those others to whom the evil is done. Then conspicuous forgiveness becomes a kind of sadism, an additional burden to bear for those to whom the evil was done: for as I know from clinical experience with my patients, the lack of proper punishment of the perpetrators of evil is itself a punishment of the victims of it, a punishment that is often long-lasting and even rather like a life sentence. This is because it removes from the victims all confidence that there is justice in the world or that anybody cares what happens to them. Their experiences and their feelings are of no account; they (the people who have them) are nothing, no more than insects under the feet of society.

It seems to me that mercy and forgiveness are often mistaken for one another. A judge may properly be merciful to those who come before him, indeed he must be so often if he is to keep his sentences within civilised bounds, such being the deserts of most wicked among us (quite apart from the fact that all of us require mercy on many occasions). But he cannot properly say 'I forgive you for what you did to Mrs Smith.' Only Mrs Smith can forgive what the accused did to her.

And what if Mrs Smith does forgive the accused, what then? At least once the law is involved, nothing much, at least where due process is concerned: because it has long been a principle that the offence by the perpetrator is not against her alone, but against society as a whole. She has no more right to demand a light punishment than a heavy one. When Bacon said that the law ought to weed out revenge, he might also have added that it should weed out forgiveness. Mercy is another matter.

Where forgiveness is often (not always) better than vengefulness is in its effect on the life of the victim. As it happens, my dream notwithstanding, I am not a very vengeful person, if only because I am too inconsistent, my attention too easily diverted by other things, to prosecute a vendetta efficiently or with determination. There have been only two or three people in my life against whom I have harboured vengeful feelings for more than a day or two, and recently I addressed a meeting at which I thought one of them might attend. I had long dreamed of humiliating him in public, as he did once me in circumstances in which I could not retort; this was twenty years ago at least, and revenge is a dish best eaten cold. But in fact I found that my desire had now completely evaporated and I was glad that it had. I can't say that this desire to be revenged on him had played a very large part in my mental life, it came into my mind perhaps once a year, and then only briefly; but nonetheless I was pleased to discover that I no longer felt it at all. He must by now have been more than eighty, and there ought to be a psychological equivalent of the statute of limitations.

What makes vengefulness so difficult to eradicate from the human heart is that it is so enjoyable to indulge it in the privacy of one's thoughts. There one can indulge in things whose attraction it would be impolitic to avow, at least if one moves in tolerably civilised society. In the fastnesses of one's thoughts, but nowhere else, one can visit upon the perpetrator precisely what he deserves. Fortunately, few people have the courage of their sadism.

Like most human traits, vengefulness and forgivingness grow stronger with habit. What starts out as an ideology can thus become a trait of character, good or bad as the ideology might be. Hatred, I have found, needs rehearsal and practice to keep it alive, otherwise it tends to attenuate, like germs passed though guinea pigs. Alas, hatred can so easily give meaning to life, especially in the absence of any other.

Oddly enough, firm punishment after due process should reduce the level of vengefulness in society rather than increase it. Man is vengeful by nature, inclined to lash out at those who do him wrong; but this tendency, inglorious as it might be, is reduced by an assurance that the wrongdoer will come to justice, even if it is justice tempered by mercy according to mitigating circumstances. Where, however, there is no such justice, private vengefulness flourishes.

As soon as I woke from my dream, while it was still half-reality in my mind, I worried that I was more likely to suffer punishment for having caught the assailant's fingers in the window than was the assailant for having grabbed me by the collar in the first place. It is said that a drowning man recapitulates his whole life in his mind in an instant; in this case, I saw in a like instant an entire future court case against me, a mixture of civil and criminal proceedings.

The law in England, at least, requires that a person defend himself with a reasonable, which is to say the least, degree of violence appropriate to the situation. It is no defence against a charge of murder, for example, that the victim pushed ahead of you in a queue, even if he shouldn't have done so. And in my oneiric state, I already heard counsel for my assailant asking me whether I had come to any actual harm because his client had grabbed my collar, how I knew that he meant me harm, whether I had asked him first what he was doing before crushing his fingers (he was a pianist and now he would never play again). Did I indeed plan to drag him down the road by his fingers, in effect amputating them as if indulging in an updated but fundamentally mediaeval form of punishment? By what right did I do this, was I not a brute? My assailant's life was ruined, in fact he was only attempting to beg, not to attack me. I owed him a substantial amount of damages.

My reply, of course, would be that it was all very well for counsel to say that I should have made proper enquiries as to the purpose and motives of my assailant, but when one is grabbed by the collar in the dead of night by an unseen person, one naturally assumes the worst. How was I to know that the assailant was not armed, that he was not intending to kill me? Such situations are not best suited to a disinterested enquiry after truth; one has to react quickly. If the law supposes that one has the time and leisure in such circumstances to find out what is really happening, and to respond to it proportionately, then the law, to quote Mr Bumble, is an ass, an idiot.

I can't really say when I had these thoughts, whether I woke or slept, or how long it took me to think them. It gradually dawned on me, in fact, that I required to go to the lavatory, but I suppose that that explanation of my nightmare would not satisfy a psychoanalyst. And though I do not much believe in the deeper meaning of dreams, I cannot help but reflect that the thoughts that this dream aroused were of some slight significance, in that they demonstrated how deeply ingrained has become the fear of litigation in modern man (assuming that I am representative of modern man). Though I have only once been sued, by a man whose suit was thrown out as vexatious by the courts even before I came anywhere near to trial, and who subsequently went on to murder (his mother, I think it was), I clearly have absorbed a fear that the civil law might one day ruin me. I once read a book by a woman who cleverly collected dreams under the Third Reich. How common, I wonder, in an increasingly litigious society, are dreams, that is to say nightmares, of being sued?

8
Spider Man

THIS YEAR has been very bad for butterflies, at least at my house in France. Normally they dance around the lavender in clouds, but this year there have been very few. Why this should be I do not know: one is inclined these days to ascribe every change in nature, especially undesirable or unwanted, to global warming.

It is curious how people's attitude to the existence of a supposedly empirical phenomenon depends so completely on their political outlook. It is as if policy determined facts and not facts policy. If people are against big government they tend to deny that there is any such phenomenon; if they are for big government they tend to regard it as established fact and equate those who deny its existence with Holocaust deniers.

I have not followed the debate very closely: frankly, it bores me even though the fate of the world is at stake. The fate of the world is too large a thing to engage my interest for very long: give me a convoluted crime any day, *I can read about that forever*. But in so far as the debate impinges on my consciousness at all, it seems to boil down to a few questions:

Is global warming taking place?

If it is taking place, is it caused by Man's activity?

If it is taking place, is it necessarily a wholly bad thing?

If it is a bad thing on balance, and is caused by Man's activity, what should be done about it?

If it is taking place, but is not the result of Man's activity what should we do about it?

Are the proposed cures worse than the disease?

My problem is that, not knowing anything about climate except that sometimes it is too hot for me and sometimes too cold, sometimes too windy and sometimes too still, but rarely just right, I am at the mercy of the last expert I hear. When someone says that the concept of global warming is suspect from the outset because there is no way of measuring the temperature of the earth as a whole, and anyway such measurements as have been made do not demonstrate, even in their own terms, any tendency to global warming, what am I supposed to think? What am I supposed to think when I see pictures, incontrovertible, of glaciers and ice caps melting? In practice what I do is to think of something else entirely, the lazy man's way out of any dilemma.

But while it has been a very bad year for butterflies, it has been a very good one for spiders—and flies (perhaps these two facts are dialectically related, though while I can see how flies might bring forth spiders, I cannot see how spiders bring forth flies). When I arrived back at my house after an absence of a few months, I thought I had stumbled upon the French National Spider Reserve, so many were there inside and outside the house.

I don't actually like spiders very much, though I recognise their role in keeping flies down. If I am honest I am a tiny bit afraid of them, though of course I do not girlishly run away from them or utter screams when I see one (this year, that is just as well, I would be hoarse by now). I can pick them up with my hands when called upon to do so, but I would really rather not.

This is somewhat odd, because I love beetles and other insects. What is it about spiders that so commonly inspires fear? In Australia, where they have so many dangerous species, fear is to a degree rational; but my faint fear of them is not allayed, as it ought to be, by knowledge the fact that in Europe spiders are very rarely dangerous. That spiders have eight legs whereas insects have only six surely cannot account for my frisson of fear. Why should two legs extra make any difference? (On the other hand, I find the *Myriapoda*, the many-legged creatures such as centipedes and millipedes, utterly repellent. I keep finding *Scutigera coleoptrata*, the Mediterranean house centipede which has fifteen pairs of legs, in my French bathtub, and am inhibited from washing it angrily down the plughole only by a vague respect for life in general and disgust at enjoyment of its suffering, if 'suffering' is the word for its struggles against the tide of water that to it would be a Tsunami; so instead of washing it away I shovel it on to a piece of paper and defenestrate it, a much more humane method of disposal. How its legs make me shudder as their contract in co-ordinated waves! And yet again, I am disgusted by worms, both segmented and unsegmented, which have no legs at all. It seems that creatures, to please me, must have the right number of legs, between two and six. This, of course, is a necessary condition, though not a sufficient one. Hyenas, hornets, cockroaches and many people do not please me.)

There is something peculiarly unpleasant about the sensation of an unseen thread of a spider's web brushing into one's face, and this year I experienced it many times as I walked in my house and garden, far more than ever before. (I don't much care for the sensation of cold used tea-bags on the skin, either.) I know that the thread which the spider spins, or rather excretes, is a marvellous thing, the strongest fibre known to Man, the strongest fibre in the universe: I tested such a fibre that had been spun between the two branches of a bush and was amazed by how hard I could pull one of the branches toward me without breaking the fibre. Even more unpleasant than bumping with one's face into a spider's web is the removal of spiders' webs from the brush one has used to clean the corners of the room, the casements, the bookshelves and so forth. It is difficult to do so: the web sticks unpleasantly to one's fingers as if one were a prey, and won't leave the brush either.

I am not alone in my disgust at spiders' webs. Horror films often use spiders' webs as a metonym for a sinister place. What I cannot quite disentangle in my mind (no pun intended) is why the sensation of the web should be so disagreeable, to the point of being horrible and even frightening. Is it the tactile sensation itself or the arachnoid association of that sensation that revolts us? I suppose an experiment could be done to elucidate the matter, if anyone thought it worth elucidating: a person could be made to come into contact alternately with a spider's web and something made to feel like a spider's web without knowing which was which. If his disgust was equal, but greater when he knew when he was in contact with a real spider's web, it would be the anti-spider culture in which he had been raised rather than the sensation itself that caused his disgust. On the other hand, it might be that our tendency to disgust of spiders' webs is inborn, as the chimpanzee's fear of snakes is said to be.

A long time ago, in my intellectual youth, I read a book called *Purity and Danger*, by the anthropologist Mary Douglas, about the way in which we humans divide into the clean and the unclean. This is a question related to that of the reasons that some animals attract and others repel. Unfortunately I did not understand the book at the time, which may not have been entirely my fault since, in a preface to a subsequent edition, the author wrote, 'the book would have been better received if it had been clearer;' but I took from it an impression that has lasted ever since, namely that our classification into the pure and the impure, the clean and the unclean, the attractive and unattractive, partakes of much more than merely rational considerations. I know, for example, that my dislike of cockroaches has little to do with their capacity to spread disease. (One senses a certain reluctance in publications devoted to pests to admit that the role of cockroaches in spreading disease is a relatively minor one at worst, that no specific epidemic outbreak has ever been proved to have been caused by them, and that the fear that they might spread disease is of the 'it stands to reason' variety because they have been found to carry pathogenic germs on their bodies. But this 'it stands to reason' kind of argument in medicine is often false, and what stands to reason is often not in fact the case; but still we feel that creatures so uniformly reviled, that crunch horribly under the shoe when stepped upon, ought, if there were any justice in the world, to be important carriers of disease.) In the case of cockroaches, it is perhaps the fear of being overrun by them that haunts us; and their resistance to being exterminated by us is an insult to our giant intelligence. They are regarded as primitive even by insect standards, and yet they outwit us: three quarters of all American homes have them. It is not the meek who will inherit the earth but the cockroaches.

What repels us can also fascinate us. I am repelled by snakes but also drawn to them: I don't think I could ever pass one by without approaching it, even if I knew it to be highly dangerous. Indeed, the danger would only encourage me to approach nearer, as a kind of test of character (mine, not the snake's). This reminds me of an essay, titled *Cigarettes Are Sublime*, by Simon Leys, the wonderful Belgian sinologist and literary essayist who lived most of his adult life in Australia and who has just died (he was my hero). 'Every time I see one of those threatening labels on a packet of cigarettes,' he wrote, 'I feel seriously tempted to start smoking again.'

In fact, I have idled away several hours this summer watching outdoor spiders. For example, near one blackberry bush where I gather blackberries (another way of putting off work, under the pretext that I am thereby living the natural life), a very large yellow, black and white striped spider has been eating a handsome dragonfly caught in its—actually her—web. I watched this Argiope spider vibrating ecstatically and sucking the juices from this large creature. By the next day the prey was gone from her web, whether entirely eaten or otherwise disposed of I cannot say. Certainly, the spider looked fatter the next day.

Perhaps more sinister, if Nature can ever be sinister, was the disappearance from the web of her husband, a comparatively small arachnid of, if I may so put it, more spidery physique. It is well known that female Argiope spiders eat their husbands, and perhaps this accounted for some of my spider's increased size the following day.

Near the verandah table on which I write is a bush in which a funnel web spider has spun its web (the funnel web spiders are out in astonishing force this year). These spiders spin a web with a funnel into which they retreat either for safety or to eat their prey, which they drag into it so that they can consume it in private.

Can spiders learn? It seems to me that they can, but perhaps I am deceiving myself. At first when I approached the web the spider would dart immediately into the depths of its funnel, like an ostrich burying its head in the sand. But gradually, over the succeeding days, it became less timid, and now does not do so unless I actually touch the web. It has learned that if I was not exactly a spider's best friend, neither was I its worst enemy.

To return to the male-eating Argiope. In his preface to Richard Dawkins' famous first book, the great evolutionary biologist, Robert Trivers, wrote that study of the social ants, wasps and bees had conclusively demonstrated that there was no genetic basis for inequality of the sexes. I wonder when the first wife-killer will argue in his defence that, in killing his wife, and having studied the behaviour of Argiope spiders, he was only acting pre-emptively, to prevent his own death; or a husband-killing wife, having also studied the behaviour of Argiope spiders, she was only acting true to biological form, and was therefore not responsible for her behaviour.

9
Serial Killers and Serial Explanations

A FRIEND OF MINE, who shall of course remain anonymous, is a great expert on the pharmacological aspects of serial killing by doctors and nurses. The cases are not many, but they are dramatic; and in the near future he will appear as an expert witness for the prosecution in a case in which a nurse is accused of killing several patients by poison. I am thinking of attending the trial to write about it.

If the accused is found guilty, or rather if the accused actually committed the crimes with which he is charged (regrettably not always quite the same thing), he acted with an unusual degree of cunning, having left his defence many possible avenues of escape. He also seems not to have had any motive apart from such strange pleasure as he might have derived from the act of killing. Perhaps he was as disinterested in the pursuit of evil as Kant's good person is in pursuit of good.

I have not had much to do personally with medical serial killers, either doctors or nurses, but shortly after the notorious case in England of a nurse called Beverley Allitt, who killed several babies by various means and was revealed later to have suffered herself from Munchausen syndrome, I was asked by the hospital in which I was working to examine a nurse working there who also suffered from, or perhaps I should say behaved as someone suffering from, Munchausen syndrome. (This is an extraordinary pattern of behaviour in which a person goes from hospital to hospital complaining of a variety of symptoms carefully chosen to signify possible serious underlying pathology, disprovable only by elaborate tests and procedures, and sometimes operations. Such a person may use up an immense quantity of medical time, energy and resources: the *British Medical Journal* once published a paper by a doctor who traced the path of a particularly prolific attender at public hospitals, and worked out that he had cost the taxpayer $17 million since he began what can only be called his career. More than once in my hospital I was able by detective work to uncover the identity of such a patient—they usually go under false names, they claim that their relatives are dead, to have just returned from abroad etc., so as to make themselves as untraceable as possible —and then, having been seriously incapacitated only moments before, rush out of the hospital when exposed as Munchausen patients, angrily swearing and cursing, sometimes threatening revenge, as if the exposure of their lies were an act of cruelty, as if their rights had been infringed. No wrongdoing is beyond the reach of self-righteousness.)

The hospital management was naturally anxious that it did not have another Beverley Allitt on its hands, and asked me to pronounce on this difficult matter. Was the nurse dangerous, or was she not? I could quite see why the hospital management was anxious about it, perhaps not so much for the safety of the patients as to avoid the vilification of themselves that would surely ensue if they permitted a serial killer to work in the hospital, a nurse known to have Munchausen syndrome. By asking me, moreover, they could deflect blame on to me if things went wrong. This is the great secret of the science of management.

The nurse, as far as anyone could tell, had done nothing wrong in the hospital—yet. My own view is that Munchausen syndrome is a form of fraud, for whatever strange compulsion the person with it may feel under, his behaviour in actually seeking admission to hospitals is perfectly conscious: he claims to have what he knows that he does not have. However, the nurse had been convicted of nothing, so could not be dismissed on grounds of criminal record. Moreover, there was a flaw in the logic which supposes that if all xs are ys, then all ys must be xs. So even if it were true that all serial killer nurses suffered from, or behaved like people with, Munchausen syndrome, it would not follow that all nurses who suffered from Munchausen syndrome were serial killers—unless there were a perfect overlap and coincidence between the two, which there is not.

Suppose (purely for the sake of argument) that half of nurses with Munchausen syndrome were serial killers of patients, what then? One can see that there would be a conflict between the rights of society and those of the individual. If the nurse were dismissed on the grounds of the high statistical risk that she posed, she might justly complain that she was being punished for what she had not done, for what she might do. She was still innocent both in law and in fact. But who would want to go, or want his loved ones to go, to a hospital where a nurse with a fifty per cent chance of becoming a serial killer was employed?

Suppose again, using the same notional statistics, that a person who acknowledged that she had Munchausen's syndrome applied for a job as a nurse to a hospital. Should she be rejected? Most people would say that she should, but if Munchausen is accepted as a bona fide disability, this would be to discriminate against her on grounds that are now forbidden by law. We are on the horns of a dilemma: either we treat her as an individual, or as a member of a group. If we treat her as an individual we defy common sense and employ her because there is nothing against her personally; but if we treat her as a member of a group and not as an individual we are in effect allowing discrimination of the kind which is commonly denounced as morally reprehensible.

In fact, it is inevitable that we discriminate in some situations and for some purposes, whether or not we do so in and for others. An airline, for example, that knowingly employed a drug addict as a pilot would be culpable; but in America it is now illegal for insurance companies to discriminate against addicts because addiction must be treated as a disease like any other.

Be this all as it may, I advised the hospital to keep a particularly sharp eye out for any unexplained medical crises, ending in death or not, that occurred on the ward in which this nurse was working. She should be suspended at the first suspicion, while investigations were carried out; but in the event, no such action was ever necessary. Whether the mere fact of having been sent to me deterred her—for of course serial killers act under conscious control—or whether she had never had any propensity to serial killing I shall never know, for it is unknowable; but of course I like to think that I averted an infamous episode, having had few occasions in my life to be a hero.

In preparation for my future attendance at the trial of the alleged serially-killing nurse, I decided to read about healthcare serial killers, and found a book by a forensic psychologist with the title *Inside the Minds of Healthcare Serial Killers*. For like almost everyone else, I am prey to the illusion that if only I study or read enough about a certain kind of behaviour, I will come to 'understand' it better. One might almost call this the mirage of understanding: it shimmers enticingly in the distance, but however far you go, it remains just as distant.

The book turned out to be mainly a descriptive compendium of cases, but as for explanation, I found it not. As we shall see, I do not blame the author, Katherine Ramsland, for this, as human behaviour is that which passeth understanding, at least by humans; perhaps there are superior beings somewhere in the universe who could understand us as we understand the laws of motion, but until then we are stuck with incomprehension, even about what understanding would be, let alone understanding itself. In other words, we have not merely incomprehension, but meta-incomprehension.

The book contains a brief historical survey of healthcare serial killers, starting in the mid-nineteenth century. Perhaps until then doctors and nurses killed their patients only by accident (George Washington perhaps among them), but as the pharmacopoeia expanded, so did opportunities to act upon dark desires. And the appetite grows with feeding.

Whether there are more healthcare serial killers than there were a few years or decades ago would, as usual, not be an easy question to answer. Publicity has given rise to awareness, the first step in detection, but it may also have given rise to emulation and even competition to be the worst of the worst. I have known people who, not having the talent to be the best at anything creditable, have settled on trying to be the worst at something discreditable: and that demand not so much talent as determination.

A rage for publicity or fame has certainly been a motive for some such killers, but certainly not all; many have done their level best to keep their depredations as hidden as possible. This brings us to a difficult question, that of the healthcare serial-killer. Is the infamous Dr Petiot, for example, a healthcare serial killer or not? Certain he was a doctor, and certainly he was a serial killer; but what he used to do during the Occupation of Paris was to lure rich Jews to his house where he would tell them that, as a member of the Resistance, and in return for their possessions for expenses, he would be able to smuggle them out to neutral countries. They would duly arrive with their possessions, when he would gas them—he had a peephole to observe them dying—and then keep the possessions for himself. Was he a healthcare serial killer or not? I would say not, because his killing was not an extension of his medical practice.

Is serial-killing by healthcare staff a single phenomenon, susceptible to a single explanation, when some do it for gain, others for thrills, yet others for sexual gratification, some for fame or notoriety, and some for no discernible reason at all? Is there a golden thread running through these crimes?

But even if there were, would it help us? Would we ever be able to say, 'Ah, now at last I understand'?

I do not think so. One of the most notorious medical serial killers of all time was Dr Harold Shipman. He may have killed up to 280 of his patients; we will never be sure how many. He never confessed, at least not to anyone whose word can be trusted, and never gave a reason for his behaviour. He put into practice the advice to politicians, 'Never apologise, never explain.'

His victims were mainly old, or oldish, ladies, most of them in good health for their age. Since he explained nothing himself, sifters in his biography sought explanations for themselves. One of the most commonly cited facts of his life is that he witnessed his mother die slowly and excruciatingly of cancer when he was 17 years old. A somewhat lonely young man, his mother was his main support and best friend. Here is what Katherine Ramsland has to say:

> Harold Shipman took care of his mother as she died. It's possible that as [he] began to kill patients, [he] found some measure of relief from anxiety when [he] exercised this form of control – not just over another person but also over their environments.

I do not blame the author for the almost comical inadequacy of this supposed 'explanation;' quite apart from any difficulty in understanding why killing should reduce anxiety more than raise it, the effect is grossly, even ludicrously, disproportionate to the presumptive cause. For every Shipman, there must be a thousand men who have seen their mothers die. But I have nothing better to propose, and I doubt that I would even if I were to devote the whole of my life to studying the case.

The fact is that explanation is a holy grail: no matter how long sought it is never found. F. H. Bradley said that metaphysics is the finding of bad reasons for what we believe on instinct, but he added that search for such reasons is no less a part of human nature for that. So it is with human behaviour. We shall never explain it; we shall never cease trying to explain it.

10
The Meaning of Life

IT ALWAYS intrigued me when I practised as a doctor to observe how Man is always but a slight injury or biochemical disturbance away from paranoia. It is almost as if paranoia were always bubbling away under the smooth surface of normal social relations, like lava below the earth's crust, waiting just some slight crack or fissure for the opportunity to emerge and cover everything. The list of possible physiological causes of paranoia is legion.

No doubt the evolutionary biologists (or should I say the biologists of evolution?) have an explanation—as they have an explanation for everything. The ability instantly to explain everything and its opposite, for example why one species should be monogamous while another, apparently very similar, should indulge in the utmost promiscuity, is usually taken not as a strength but as a weakness in a theory; moreover the element of circularity in the theory of natural selection, that animals survive in greater numbers because they are better fit to survive in such numbers, as measured by the numbers in which they actually *do* survive, has struck many people. And yet Darwinian theory is clearly not empty, especially since the advent of modern genetics. The trouble comes, I think, when the theory is extended beyond its field of application or competence.

Anyway, it is easy to see that in a biosphere plentifully supplied with enemies, competitors (even if the competitors are genes, as some claim, rather than organisms), predators, parasites, etc., it is obvious that a paranoid stance, if not paranoia itself, might be advantageous. That is why every creature, every creature at any rate than can be said truly to have behaviour, exhibits nervousness. Even the king of the jungle has dethronement to fear; the price of life is eternal vigilance (and even then it's not guaranteed).

So perhaps it is non-paranoia rather than paranoia that needs to be explained, just as it is wealth and not poverty than stands in need of explanation. How is it that I have been able (so far) to go through life on the assumption that no one is trying to do me down, that no enemies are lurking for me anywhere, and that I have nothing to worry about even when people respond in an insulting fashion to things that I have written? When I can't get through to speak to anyone at my bank, my telephone or electricity company, I know that they have nothing against me: it is simply that they are trying to provide the least possible service for the maximum of charges. This is not paranoia, it is observable fact, or at least reasonable inference from observable fact.

Another source of human paranoia—I am not now talking of that which is produced by physiological disturbance—is the assumption that other people's thoughts are similar to ours, that is to say the thoughts to which we are especially and uniquely privy. Here I do indeed assume, dear reader, that you are like me, and that you have thoughts that you feel you ought not to have (I don't need to enumerate them, I think, but even if I did need to do so I wouldn't), thoughts that are disguised or not acted upon. I know that I habitually play the hypocrite and since I assume that you are like me, I assume that you too often play the hypocrite (thank goodness). It means that if I have hostile thoughts towards others that I never express, others must have hostile thoughts towards me that they never express. To suppose otherwise is to suppose that I am much worse than, or completely different from, others, which naturally I am reluctant to do. But this means that in a world which is, or might be, full of hostile thoughts towards us that we know nothing about, it is easy, if we dwell upon the situation, to become paranoid.

And because our thoughts and actions are so deeply impregnated with intention and purpose, we over-ascribe intention and purpose elsewhere, not only to our fellow humans, but to all kinds of creatures and even to inanimate objects. Which of us, for example, has never tripped over a stone or stubbed his toe on it, and not at least *thought* of revenging himself upon it for the indignity or pain it has inflicted on us? I have actually done so, though usually with disastrous effect: to stub one's toe on a stone once may be regarded as a misfortune, but to kick it in rage a second time looks like stupidity.

Of course we know perfectly well that the stone has no intentions or purposes, let alone the ability to suffer if we kick it or hurl into the distance it as far as we can, but yet we still feel that it did it on purpose: that is to say, deliberately put itself in the way of our foot just as it knew we were coming. I don't resort to swearing very much, and I should guess that on half the occasions that I do so it is to insult and otherwise humiliate inanimate objects.

With animate beings, not surprisingly, we go further: we endow them with personalities and characters. We do this almost without thinking, much as we automatically ascribe characteristics to people's faces without a separate thought-process, such as 'I wonder what that scar down the side of his cheek means?'

The other day I was driving on a small road in some woods when an eagle suddenly glided majestically in front of the car. I at once gave it a character, and try as I might I cannot disabuse myself of it, though I know it to be preposterous.

The eagle (I thought) was a serious bird, without a sense of humour and not much fun to be with; it had no small talk. It looked frightfully earnest, or serious rather (not the same thing, alas), and utterly concentrated on its own affairs, not to be diverted from them. It was also an upright and implacable bird—upright in the moral sense—and if it caught little animals it was only for their own good, to impose order on their anarchic ways, and to punish them for foolishness in running about.

That same evening a little sparrow flew through the window into my bedroom, landed on the top of my Louis Seize wardrobe and chirruped a little. Then he flew to the headboard of my bed and chirruped a bit more. Then, as if he had just come to wish me good evening, he flew out of the window again.

What a nice, friendly, amusing little chap he was! I think he had a sense of humour. He gave me a sense of company. Where the eagle was majestical, he was down to earth, perhaps a little ironical. He was full of life and I wished he had stayed longer (the eagle, if he ever condescended to enter my house, would not deign to talk to me and would outstay his welcome, like a boring hospital visitor, and yet he would manage to convey that the fault was mine). Of course, I know nothing real of the habits of sparrows and perhaps they are ferociously competitive birds, who like nothing better than to take the food out of each other's beaks and ruin each other's nests out of evolutionary spite; but I prefer to think that my sparrow liked me as much as I liked him.

Outside my kitchen door there is a terrace where, in the summer, the lizards play—and fight. They are not large lizards, maybe four or five inches long, and some of those inches mere tail. Sometimes I see them catch a large ant and crunch it in their jaws. At a certain time of year though, they fight ferociously, curling up and wrestling with one another, rolling around with considerable violence (considering their size).

They desist from time to time in their struggle and stand staring at one another, breathing very fast. I know their brains are very small and of the most primitive, but I find it hard to believe that they are not very angry with each other, almost morally indignant. Then, after a short break, between the rounds as it were, they start again.

I can usually tell in advance who is going to win. One of the two seems almost to be reticent, or more on the defensive; he is fighting not so much to win (he knows that he won't), but for the sake of honour. To retire from the field without having put up a fight would be a fatal blow to his self-esteem. By the time he runs away, he (I assume it is a he) can honestly say to his wife, when she disparagingly asks him whether he is a lizard or a mouse, that he is a lizard. He has nothing to be ashamed of.

The victor, usually the larger of the two, looks extremely pleased with himself as the sole occupant of the paving stone, his opponent having slunk away in defeat. The victor's head is raised, he is the monarch of all he surveys. I feel like Gulliver as he watched the battle between Lilliput and Blefescu. I could easily crush the proud victor of the saurian fight with one tramp of my foot and put an end to his ridiculous and intolerable pride: but then I think how easily crushed I could be, and I reprove myself.

Just beyond the terrace is a bed of lavender, and here, during the season, I can happily spend hours (well, minutes at any rate) looking at the butterflies and other insects that visit the flowers constantly. I particularly like the humming-bird moths, for they are not only beautiful but somehow their darting movements from one flower to another (that makes it difficult to catch them on camera, or rather difficult for me to catch them on camera) somehow symbolise the bittersweet transience of life.

Several different kinds of bees visit the lavender, which seems as a consequence to emit a cheerful buzzing, nothing loud or vulgar but pleasing on the ear. One might almost think the lavender a kind of heaven but, alas, there lurks within it an evil snow white spider that turns it into a hell for a small number of bees. This spider looks like something from a science fiction film, it whiteness somehow being sinister where that of the butterflies is charming.

This spider is much smaller than the bees; he (or she) spins no web but rather hides and then pounces, sticking its venomous palps (for such I suppose they must be) into the bee and paralysing it. Then it sticks to the bee, which hangs helpless from the lavender in its grip, while the latter sucks the life juices out of it and turns it into a dried exoskeleton.

Disgusting! If I could rescue a bee in this situation I would, but unfortunately the bees have always been dead by the time I reach them. It is too late. Besides, though I attribute evil to the spider and goodness to the bees, I also have the semi-pagan feeling that Nature must know best, and to interfere with the activities of the spiders would be somehow to upset Nature's carefully thought-out balance.

But, on the other hand, do not the spiders know that there is a world-wide bee crisis, a shortage of bees! Could they not, should they not, fix on other prey, less ecologically important, than bees? There are plenty of beetles around, for example. Selfish, selfish spiders! They are like men, thoughtlessly using up the resources of the world for their own current convenience, with ne'er a thought for the morrow.

On the one hand I know perfectly well that this habit of infusing meaning, intention and purpose into the living world around me is not a guide to the literal truth of that world; spiders are not wicked any more than bees are good, or lizards triumphant. But I should nevertheless feel I had lost something important if, as is very unlikely, I ever managed to expunge this way of thinking entirely from my mind. The strange thing is that I have noticed that the hardest of hard-line evolutionists never quite manage it either. They, too, describe the world by reference to function, purpose and intention. I suppose they would say we have evolved to be like this.

11
Zerbran at the Bozar

MY WIFE and I decided to go to Brussels from Paris for the day to see the Zurburán exhibition at the Palais des Beaux-Arts. The train, however, would have cost us $450, and a flight even more, though the distance is not great. Those are the kind of prices paid by businessmen and bureaucrats (or should I say by taxpayers on behalf of bureaucrats?), to whom they mean nothing, not by art-lovers such as we. We almost gave up.

But by one of those coincidences that make you sometimes believe in divine providence, I happened on an article in the newspaper on the very day we looked at prices to go to Brussels on the internet. It was about a young Frenchman, Frédéric Mazilla, who had founded a company called BlaBlaCar. The idea came to him one Christmas when he wanted to go home to a provincial city from Paris. The trains were full and so he had to drive. He noticed en route that thousands of cars were driving in the same direction as he, but that most of them were empty apart from the driver. A website offering lifts to people who wanted to travel from people who were going anyway to the same destination would kill several birds with one stone: it would assist the drivers and the passengers, and reduce waste.

The drivers are not professionals: there are maximum charges according to the respective distances of the trips, and the drivers do not make a profit, they simply get their expenses back. The site allows passengers to comment on the drivers in whose cars they have travelled. Millions of people a year in Europe now use the site, of whose existence I had not previously been aware: a valuable lesson in how a large-scale development may now occur in our societies without one being aware of it.

It would cost us $120 for a round trip using BlaBlaCar, and so we booked. I would still have preferred to go by train, but I managed to persuade myself that it was an adventure and that the journey in the car would add something to the day.

And so, in a way, it proved, especially on the outward journey. When I had told my friends that we were taking BlaBlaCar they thought we were mad, or at least foolhardy; what if the driver were a serial killer? It is an interesting reflection upon the fear that reigns in our society that thoughts of serial killers came instantaneously to everyone's mind on learning of our trip, extremely rare though serial killers are. The only way to overcome unreasonable mistrust, and to re-establish trust, is to act trustingly.

It happened that our drivers on this occasion were a couple in their early sixties on their way to visit their daughter in Brussels. They were taking her vegetables from their garden—mainly cauliflowers which, *en masse*, exude quite a strong acrid smell (I had not realised this before, being only a small-scale consumer of cauliflower, so I learned something at once). Fortunately there is a physiological law—another sign of divine providence?—according to which awareness of a stimulus declines as it is prolonged. Before long, the odour disappeared of its own accord.

Unfortunately, a large truck had caught fire on the highway we were taking northwards out of Paris and it took us more than two hours to go about twenty miles. This, however, was not without its compensations (of a kind): for it allowed us to see what we should otherwise have sped past without seeing, or noticing, namely the *bidonvilles,* the settlements of corrugated iron, plastic sheeting and concrete tiles, that have recently sprung up on wasteland by the highway on the outskirts of Paris, just beyond the roadside fringes of bushes and small trees. I say 'sprung up,' but really I should have said 'been erected,' for of course they did not grow by force of nature, they were erected by hand of Man. They were what one expects to see in rapidly-urbanising Third World countries, not in France nowadays. They were not a pleasing sight.

From the look of the inhabitants, they were gypsies from Eastern Europe. They had beaten-up old white vans and cars, and they were the kind of people who have an infinite supply of broken fridges and cookers to leave behind them when they go. The women were dressed in long colourful skirts, the men in American ghetto costume.

Several of the *bidonvilles* have been abandoned or razed, making it look as though an army with a scorched-earth policy had recently passed through; the police were busy in one of the still-inhabited settlements. My reaction to these settlements was that of the average citizen, namely one of irritation and disgust; I associated them with crime, violence and intimidation; and the fact is that no one, whatever his political principles, wants such a settlement anywhere near his own home. Gypsies should be free to do as they like, but please God not near me: that is the lazy thought of most people in Europe. Of course, everyone is at least subliminally aware of the Nazi attempt to exterminate the gypsies which has made the exertion of authority over them, let alone high-handedness with them, politically and psychologically near impossible; and as we drove on, very slowly, I averted not so much my gaze as my thoughts from the problem, as being impossible to solve within the bounds of the ethically permissible. I preferred to think of Zurburán.

As we approached the site of the accident we were diverted from the highway on to another road. We were now being denied the spectacle of a large burnt-out vehicle which might have been another slight compensation for our unpleasantly wasted time. We all felt cheated, a proof of an essential difference between Man and the animals: Man is the only creature capable of prurience.

We reached Brussels. The centre is a bourgeois city gone thoroughly to seed. It is dirty and unswept, the houses, once instinct with bourgeois pride and prosperity, are neglected. About half the women, it seemed, wore the scarf proclaiming them Moslem—in actual fact, 25 per cent of the population of Brussels, unadjusted for age, is Moslem—and were dressed modestly, that is to say in a fashion that made them look like females poured into sacks, as unbecoming a costume as it would be possible to design. (Not all Moslem costumes for women are such: the salwar kameez, for example, which is often of the greatest elegance, and vastly more grateful on the eye than the way in which many western women now dress.)

We parted from our drivers at the Gare du Midi, the South Railway Station, and took a taxi to the Palais des Beaux-Arts. The driver was of Moroccan origin, and was clearly very proud of Brussels, 'three times capital,' he said, first of Belgium, then of its own region, and lastly of Europe. Given its degeneration, I am not sure I found this entirely reassuring: a capital that, despite the fact that the public sector accounts for 50 per cent of GDP, remains dirty and uncared for, and is architecturally ever more a hideous mish-mash. Many of the buildings were defaced by graffiti, the architectural equivalent of tattoos and just as idiotically egotistic. On one of walls opposite the station we saw the following slogan in Flemish:

NO ONE IS ILLEGAL

Presumably this meant that, in the opinion of the person who painted it, Belgium (and Europe) should not attempt to restrict in any way whatsoever the number of people entering it to settle. I doubt that it meant that other countries should allow Belgians (and Europeans) to settle wherever in the world they chose.

The Palais des Beaux-Arts has moved with the times. It now projects itself as the Bozar, orthography more suited to the age of text and twitter that combines youthful informality with the totalitarian tradition of language reform. But no change of name can disguise the fact that the Bozar is undoubtedly the ugliest of all the major art galleries of the world, a building in the fascist style but without the courage of its megalomania, designed as if by a pocket Albert Speer.

Of Zurburán I will one day write elsewhere; but here I will mention that the exhibition, which was not excessively well-attended (thank goodness, for it is horrible to have to peer at paintings as though through a crowd, darkly) attracted, as far as I could see, not a single non-European member of the public. And this is curious because if the museum had held an exhibition of African or Islamic art I think this would not have been so. There would, of course, have been many Europeans, but also non-Europeans, Moslems to look at Islamic art and Africans to look at African art. It has often been remarked that the Europeans, for all their military conquests and depredations, have long been the people with the deepest interest in the culture of others, and there seemed to be confirmation of this at the Bozar—though I suspect that interest in their own culture, at least their own culture of the past, is on the wane among Europeans.

We had another driver to return to Paris. He was charming, a Belgian who had at temporary job in IT in France to which he was now returning after a long weekend. His father was Congolese, his mother Romanian; he seemed completely at ease, without complexes, and described himself as a *métis*, a crossbreed.

We met him at the Gare du Midi, where we had arrived in Brussels. Having time to kill, and being hungry, we searched for somewhere to eat. There were some pretty unsavoury-looking bars where we would have been out of place among the loudly laughing and squabbling habitués. Before long we found an excellent cheap Moroccan canteen where alcohol was not served and where, as a result, quiet reigned. The staff—all men, of course—welcomed us warmly and even showered us with hospitality. The food was copious and good, and I thought of the mistaken saying, by an Italian journalist or professor I think it was, that multiculturalism is not couscous, it is the stoning of adulterers. This is wrong because multiculturalism is couscous, even if it is other things as well.

At the far end of the canteen a large flat-screen TV relayed pictures (the sound was turned off) of another crisis in Africa, hungry refugees in a camp queuing for a bowl of what looked like an appalling porridge made by an NGO on an industrial scale. The scenes, now banal, had no effect upon my appetite.

By contrast, I could not help but wonder what the lives of the men serving in this canteen were like when they went home. Where and how did they live? What, if anything, did they hope for, both for themselves and their children? Were they happy, unhappy, or something between the two? What amused, moved or angered them? These are the kind of questions that I ask myself ever more frequently when I am assisted by others in ways that I am inclined to take for granted. I think, at least I hope, that they have made me more polite, less inclined to become irritable when I am not served immediately and to my liking.

Our driver dropped us at the Porte de Bagnolet, one of the entrances to intramuros Paris. It was a fifteen minute walk from there to our flat. It was late at night, it was quite warm, and we thought it would be nice to have a cold beer when we arrived back. We stopped at a small store which, as usual in Paris, was owned by a North African. He was polite and helpful as we made a few other purchases as well. What was his life like when he shut up shop past midnight? Who would do this work if he did not?

12
Lunch Conquers All, Part I

MEN WHO bestride their academic disciplines and institutions like colossi are soon forgotten, in part because these days there are simply too many disciplines and too many institutions for them all to be remembered as they deserve and as their work merits. Names that once inspired awe or fear, or both, now evoke mere puzzlement among their successors, or at best ring the faintest of bells in the back of their minds. (Incidentally, when something rings a faint bell in the back of my mind, I feel it physically, somewhere inside my skull just above and to the left of the nape of my neck.)

Some, perhaps most, disciplines are too *recherché* for even their greatest scholars to be known to a wider public. How many of us could name a single Assyriologist, though to be an Assyriologist in the first place, let alone an eminent one, you must master of a formidable range of disciplines.

I came recently into possession of letters of two of the most eminent British psychiatrists of the twentieth century, Sir Aubrey Lewis and Eliot Slater. Sir Aubrey Lewis was the medical director (the second in its history) of the pre-eminent British psychiatric research hospital, the Maudsley, and Eliot Slater worked there too. Lewis had studied anthropology as well as medicine; and although he wrote no books as such, his erudite and influential papers were published in book form, and are still worth reading—which is not, of course, the same thing as saying that they are still read. In his time Lewis was renowned around the (psychiatric) world, and many honours were conferred on him. As for Slater, he was a polymath. An expert in the genetics of schizophrenia, he wrote a famous paper decrying the diagnosis of hysteria, showing that many people diagnosed with hysterical conversion actually turned out in the long run to have *bona fide* neurological disease (I think he was wrong). He showed the connection between temporal lobe epilepsy and schizophrenia. He was part-author of one of the best textbooks of psychiatry of his day. But he also wrote learnedly about music and the illnesses of composers, as well as about chess openings, he painted more than averagely well, and he was awarded a PhD aged 77 for his statistical work on the language of the play Edward III, showing that it was likely to be Shakespeare's.

Lewis and Slater were men of enormous intellect and energy, even if it cannot be said that they discovered much that was incontrovertible, in the last analysis the only criterion of greatness in science. But by the standards of their pygmy discipline, they were giants indeed.

It is delightful, then, to read the letters that Slater and Lewis wrote to each other, that prove (once again) that giants are not immune from pettiness, intrigue and wounded *amour propre*. At the time of Slater's letter (1948) to Lewis he was already very senior at the Maudsley, though Lewis, as director, was his superior. Slater wrote:

> Dear Lewis [in those days upper class British men addressed each other by their surnames, as Holmes did Watson and vice versa], You and I are old friends, and we are in danger of quarrelling; this is despite, on my side, warm liking, respect, and a considerable degree of gratitude for what you have personally done to help me.

Note the feline 'on my side', which indicates, to those alert to it, a sense of awareness of, and injury by, non-reciprocation. And of course there is a but in the offing, and actually the rest of the letter consists of a long elaboration of that but.

Slater continues:

> You have quarrelled with lots of other men who were your friends, and it always happens the same way. I do not think you have any natural intuition of the feelings of others [quite a handicap in a psychiatrist, one might have supposed, and therefore a deficiency the allegation of which would be especially hurtful], and so you are always doing things to wound them. If they express views which are different to yours, you see only the weaknesses in their position. You do not try to

> make allowance for them, and nearly every discussion with you becomes a battle – that is unless the other gives way entirely.

In other words, Lewis prefers triumph to truth: like Doctor Johnson, he talks for victory. The purpose of human intercourse is to establish a hierarchy of power.

The indictment continues:

> You spoke yesterday about the discontent at the Maudsley. Have you any conception that it is these traits of personality in yourself which is the principal cause of it?

One begins by now to wonder that if this is what Slater thought of those for whom he felt 'a warm liking,' what he thought of those for whom he felt a warm detestation?

Slater then gets down to a specific example:

> I should like to revert to your proposal to drop the title of Assistant Physician and to include all those with this rank among the Physicians. Have you any idea how this proposal would impress any of the Physicians?

Wounded pride could hardly be more clearly implied, but it is soon spelled out:

> The implication is that there is nothing in their professional standing to distinguish them from Assistant Physicians... [all] practically of the same status, and one immeasurably lower than yours. This is, in effect, an insult.

Slater sees behind his little game:

> There is the implication that by such an amalgamation of ranks our standing in the Hospital would be reduced, and your power correspondingly increased.

Nor was he alone (according to him) in thinking this:

> I am sure that all three Hospital Physicians... felt that this

> might be on your mind, and that the reasons you gave for your proposal did not express all your motives. Your proposal was in fact a direct frontal assault on us.

Whether secret motives are quite compatible with an allegedly direct frontal assault I leave to others to decide; but Slater is relentless:

> You refused to withdraw from your position and insisted flatly on maintaining it. Can you see how arrogant that is? It implies that our views were of no account; you must be, and we could not possible be right. It implies also that our feelings were not worth consideration. Do you seriously believe that you can never be in error? This is a quality which marks all your conduct of affairs...

Lewis could hardly have been pleased to receive such a letter, even from a soi-disant friend. He answered it, I must say, with a finesse that I found admirable.

> Dear Slater [he replied], I suppose it is salutary to know the faults our friends find in us, even if we don't recognize the picture.

That is to say, 'You are quite wrong, I'm not like that at all. I am perfect in fact.' He continues:

> I don't want to reply in kind to your chastening, or copy you in attributing rather base motives for your actions when they don't please me.

In other words, this is precisely what I am going to do, but more subtly than you did it.

> I don't question your assurance that you speak from conviction – why should I? – and I believe you are quite unaware how your arguments and actions sometimes appear to other people: but in case you interpret that as *tu quoque* stone-throwing, I can add at once that most people – including myself – seem to me to suffer from the same disability where their personal interests are involved, and weighing up

> comparative degrees of this insensitiveness is a nice calculation that I wouldn't like to make.

In other words, I am not going to resort to *ad hominem* mud-slinging – unlike you!

Having got the insults almost out of the way, Lewis then proposes—'in spite of a few things you have done that seemed to me unfriendly'—that they should deal with things in a better way:

> I would prefer to suggest friendly discussion of these things over a meal occasionally, without Maudsley company – my impression was that our fortnightly lunches, which I valued, in the earlier years of the war, fell through when Sargant started to come to them.

To understand the subtlety of this, it is necessary to explain that William Sargant was another eminent psychiatrist, a great believer of restoring people to sanity by physical methods such as insulin coma, electroshock and lobotomy. (It is an old principle of therapeutics that if you can make treatment more unpleasant than the disease, people stop complaining of the disease, even if they don't get better from it.) Indeed, Sargant was evangelical in his fervour for such treatments, and he became as notorious in some circles as he was revered in others. Certainly he bore with fortitude the deaths of his patients under his experimental treatments. But in 1944, he was co-author with Slater of a book, *An Introduction to Physical Methods of Treatment in Psychiatry*, that was to go through five editions and was the first of Slater's several books. It may be presumed, therefore, that the two were allies, so that Lewis's remark, that the lunches were not so good once Sargant came to them, might be construed as an attempt to drive a wedge between the two: in other words, divide and rule.

Then came Lewis's modest proposal:

> Will you come and have dinner with me at the Athenaeum one evening next week [the Athenaeum is the London club for distinguished men of letters, scientists and academics]? I leave it to your judgment whether before or after the next meeting of the academic Board would be better.

For a man without any 'natural instinct for the feelings of others' this was admirably subtle, though I dare say that Slater might have seen through it (I do not have the follow-up letter). He who was accused of behaving as if the views of others were of no account to him was now leaving it to his subordinate to decide something binding on them both: and there is no better way of flattering people than deferring to their decisions, even if they are only in small matters. This, of course, is the better to slip larger decisions, autocratically taken, past them.

The letters were highly literate, and one may wonder whether, in an age of instant communication, letters like them will ever be written again. But the petty querulousness of them certainly persists in the world today, or at least my experience of institutions suggests that it does. I have little doubt that both Slater and Lewis thought the matter of whether the Assistant Physicians and Physicians of the Maudsley Hospital should be lumped together as one category was of the first significance, and not just one of factional in-fighting. Perhaps they lost no sleep over it, but they probably expended much thought on it, scheming and counter-scheming, and wasting the energy of their considerable intellects on it. Clearly the matter engaged their emotions at a deep level, and yet how petty it all seems now! These men were, in point of education and intelligence, within the highest thousandth of the population, but that did not protect them from the self-obsession (disguised, of course, as matters of principle) of the other 99.9 per cent of humanity.

Needless to say, my own concerns, and I am sure those of my readers, do not partake of Slater's and Lewis' pettiness (such pettiness becomes clear only in retrospect). We do not fret, as did they, over the baubles of rank in a hierarchy, or over achieving predominance in an institution that, however illustrious in its field, was after all of small account in the history of the world. They—our concerns—are invariably matters of important abstract principle, and have nothing to do with the preservation or inflation of our *amour propre*. We are above such things.

But still I admire Lewis' sinuous letter, and his resort to lunches and dinners to smooth relations with a fractious, disgruntled and potentially dangerous colleague. I wish I knew whether the dinner at the Athenaeum actually took place, and whether it restored relations between the two men. But if I had either written or received a letter like Slater's, I would never again be quite at ease with its recipient or its author.

13
Lunch Conquers All, Part II

THERE IS no such thing as a free lunch, they say, and perhaps this is so in the abstract: but no doctor really believes it. His personal experience leads him to conclude otherwise: thanks to the pharmaceutical industry there are many free lunches, as there have been for many a long year.

As a student I loved those free lunches, indeed they were essential to my welfare and frequently staved off malnutrition if they did not quite save my life. They were available at grand rounds in the hospital and I (and my friends) gorged ourselves on them because we were so hungry. Needless to say we took no notice of what was being advertised at those lunches; we were too busy eating. And we were hungry because had spent what little money we had on champagne and other essentials, and were reduced as a consequence to existing much of the time on beer and bread and butter. Man—or at least Student—often really did live by bread alone.

What is peculiar is that the avidity for free lunches remains active in many doctors well after they have reached the stage of prosperity and the ability to afford any lunch they like from their own resources. I suppose men do not become wealthy by neglecting small economies, and doctors are not unique in their appreciation of this fact. A free lunch is therefore as attractive to the millionaire as to the pauper. And there are no more avid would-be consumers of supposedly free lunches than the contemporary English. For them, a free lunch rights any wrong, changes any enemy into a friend, and is in general devoutly to be wished, if it is not actually the *summum bonum*.

After NATO ceased bombing Serbia in 1999—the alliance was militarily humiliated in that war, for it failed by immense numbers of bombing raids even seriously to scratch the Serbian armed forces, which were hardly formidable—I suggested in a prominent British weekly journal that, now that the cruise missiles were no longer needed in the Balkans, they could usefully be turned upon some of the dreadful buildings by which our own green and pleasant land had been horribly disfigured in late years: disfigured by a symbiosis of corrupt city councillors, grasping property developers and criminally-bad architects inspired by a barbaric modernist ideology. I said in the article that everyone would have his favourite building that merited destruction by cruise missile, but that mine was the Giffard Hotel in Worcester, a concrete-clad building to gladden the heart of the Ceausescus or Le Corbusier (the latter being far worse than the former, of course, because his influence was worldwide rather than confined to a single country), right in the precincts of the city's magnificent cathedral. No single building has ever done more than this to ruin an ancient townscape once and for all, beyond possibility, while it still stands, of repair; and an acquaintance of mine remembered the elegant eighteenth-century building that was demolished to make space for it, the wonderful wooden panelling of the drawing and dining rooms being thrown into the street as so much rubbish (where my acquaintance recuperated it for nothing). No building, for purely architectural reasons, ever merited bombardment more.

The following week, the local newspaper ran a headline, MAGAZINE SAYS 'BOMB WORCESTER.' This was not quite the message I had wished to convey or, I think, the message that any sensible person would have thought I wished to convey. Local newspapers have to sell copies like any other newspapers, however, and such a headline would undoubtedly have caught the attention of the city-folk.

Shortly thereafter a local radio station asked me to explain myself to the good citizens of Worcester. Also appearing on the programme was the manager of the hotel whose destruction by bombing I had so strongly advocated. I felt a little sorry for him, for his job was to defend the indefensible. It was not a job I should have liked.

I explained why I thought the hotel should be demolished. It was a brutal eyesore and waste ground, even a pile of rubble, would be preferable to it. The manager—a perfectly pleasant young man—was asked for his response.

'What you have to remember,' he said, 'was that the hotel was built in the 1960s.'

'Yes,' I said, 'that is precisely what I am complaining of.'

It is surprising how often people think that the repetition or rephrasing of your complaint is an answer to it.

'Well,' the hapless manager said, 'have you ever been inside?'

'I don't need to go inside,' I said. 'I can see it's monstrous from the outside. Going inside will not help.'

Actually, this is not strictly true. Once you were inside it, you couldn't see its exterior, which was an inestimable advantage.

'What,' said the manager, 'if I offered you lunch?'

I admit that I was taken aback by the brazenness of the suggestion. I had not expected it.

'What's that got to do with it?' I said. 'It's a terrible building and ought to be demolished, that's all there is to it. Lunch won't alter the fact.'

Perhaps the manager thought that, if he gave me a nice free, well-lubricated lunch I would change my opinion and print a retraction in the magazine. Then the local newspaper would be able to run a headline, 'MAGAZINE NOW SAYS WORCESTER SHOULD NOT BE BOMBED.'

What struck me so forcefully about the proposition that we should have lunch was not the proposition itself, for as a man of the world I am sure that this is often how things are arranged, but that it was made in the most public way possible, over the radio, with thousands of people listening. And this could mean only one thing (other, possibly, that the manager was surpassingly stupid), namely that the manager expected that no one would notice the deeply corrupt nature of what he said because everyone thought it perfectly normal to buy people's opinions in this way, and in fact that this was the usual way opinion was formed and unformed. In other words, what the manager said was so corrupt that it was almost innocent: for where everyone is guilty, everyone is innocent. It brought to mind the title of one of J K Galbraith's books (his last, published when he was 95), *The Economics of Innocent Fraud.*

In the article in question I happened to mention also another building in another town, Shrewsbury, that I considered in urgent need of destruction. Now Shrewsbury is a very beautiful ancient town, and the building I mentioned was so transcendently awful that I alleged that the town council that permitted it to be built must have been bribed to do so. Again I was asked to explain myself on a local radio station, this time with an irate member of the council.

'Are you saying that we are corrupt?' he demanded to know, beside himself, almost, with indignation.

'Don't you understand,' I replied, 'that that is the charitable interpretation? We all like money, and if you did it for money it wouldn't be good, but we could at least understand it. But if you did it for some other reason…' Here I almost rendered myself almost speechless with the horrible thought of it. 'No,' I said, 'I can't think as ill of you as that.'

Shortly afterwards I reviewed a book for the same magazine. It was quite a good book, fluently written, but not really more than a competent scissors and paste job. It was by a doctor, and I therefore felt some professional solidarity with him. I praised the book as much as I was able while remaining within the bounds of truthfulness, and was relatively gentle in my criticisms. Some, I suppose, might have construed me as damning with faint praise, but such was not my intention; and in every book that I review that is not actively pernicious, I try to insert some words that can be torn by the publisher without too much violence or dishonesty for use as a blurb. When I started to review books many years ago it is true that I thought it would be fun to criticise slashingly and without mercy; but I soon discovered that praise was more pleasurable to bestow than was condemnation to hurl, and that unless a book was actively dishonest in some dangerous way I refrained from severity. After all, even a bad book has cost its author some considerable effort and he must believe that it has some worth or value when he sent it into the world. (The only exception was a book that the author claimed to have written in three days. I think he meant us, the readers, to be astounded by his genius: so short a time, so deep a book. I wrote that I was surprised that it took him as long to write it as that.)

No sooner was my review published than I received a letter from the author—in those days letters still existed and were written—suggesting that we must meet because we had so much in common, and inviting me to lunch at the Savoy (an expensive rendezvous in London). I was puzzled by this, for I had not written ecstatically in praise of his book, but somewhat lukewarmly. But it took me not more than a second or two to grasp what he was at: I thought he must be in the process of writing another book—my surmise turned out to be quite correct—that he thought I was likely to be asked to review. Having been lunched expensively it would have been difficult for me to write an unfavourable review, or even a non-committal one: for lunch in the Savoy creates its moral obligations. You have to be something of a swine to lunch at someone's considerable expense and not feel any obligation at all to him.

I wrote to thank him, but instead of saying that it would be wrong of me to accept, I rather cravenly made some footling excuse as if I much regretted my inability and would have liked to accept another time. And indeed, he tried it once more to invite me but then gave up. He was no fool and must have realised that my second excuse was precisely that, an excuse.

I was right that he was writing another book, and he was right that I would be asked to review it. My other surmise at the time—that his second book would not be as good as his first because he was really a one-book man, being without much imagination—also turned out to be correct. I was free to criticise it (albeit gently) as I should not have been had I lunched with him at his expense. I should have felt constrained to praise his book beyond its merit, my obligation to him personally far outweighing in my mind that to the public in the abstract. When I read very favourable reviews of this book elsewhere, I wondered how many of the reviewers he had succeeded in lunching.

Yes, lunch conquers all, more than love. When, as happens occasionally, some politician's corruption stands revealed in the press, what shocks me about it is often the trifling amount by which he has benefited and by which he had allowed himself to be corrupted. Just as it is the small insults, humiliations and acts of disdain that people have suffered rather than frightful injustices that move them to political anger and even violence, so it is small obligations that are more corrupting than large. Large sums of money transferred to a secret account are impersonal; lunch is a social event.

The doctor who tried to extract a good review from me by means of lunch was soon afterwards in trouble. He was caught with his fingers in some till or other in which they had no business to be and, though he claimed it was by inadvertence, he lost his licence to practise for a time.

In a way, I suppose, his invitation was flattering, for he obviously thought that my good opinion in print was likely to result in sales that would yield him more in royalties than the lunch would have cost him. Today, as it happens, I spoke to a publisher who, *inter alia*, said, 'Of course, reviews don't sell books.' But lunch buys reviewers.

14
How I Rwanda What You Are

IF EVER THERE WERE a competition for the most cynical remark ever made, I think François Mitterand's at the beginning of genocide in Rwanda would stand a fair chance of winning. 'In those countries down there,' he is said to have said, 'a genocide isn't too important.'

I came across this uplifting sentiment in a book that I bought at the Shoah Memorial in Paris recently, *Gêneurs de survivants!* (*Annoying Survivors!*), by Dominique Celis, a half-Rwandan woman living in Belgium. There was an exhibition at the Memorial to mark the twentieth anniversary of the genocide, perhaps the most democratic of all Twentieth Century genocides, or at any rate the one with the greatest popular participation. There were photos, recorded testimonies, even a few videos of the massacres themselves, though not too many to sicken the sensitive or satiate the sadistic. There was a pile of clothes of the massacred, from which I thought I could detect a characteristic smell (I am familiar with the smell of massacre), but my wife said that it was in my imagination. There were the instruments of genocide, from scythes and machetes to home-made mallets with which to smash skulls.

On our way to the Memorial, to pass the time in the Métro, I had been reading the *Black Book of Psychoanalysis*, an uncompromising critique of Freud and his legacy. Freud was no scientist; he was instead an unscrupulous charlatan, oscillating between wishful thinking and outright lying, a psychopathic manipulator who owed his success not to the truth but to the emptiness of his theories, the founder of a religious sect rather than of a scientific discipline, a man avid for fame and fortune only too aware that he might not achieve them by more conventional means, and an incestuous adulterer to boot. Moreover, his technique, if something as nebulous as psychoanalysis can be called a technique, was of no greater therapeutic value than exorcism, although much more expensive and a great deal less fun—except for those who desired to talk endlessly about themselves and were willing to pay someone else to listen to them or at least pretend to listen to them.

France, as well as Argentina, is the last redoubt in the world of psychoanalysis (not that this prevents the French from being world-champion psychotropic medication swallowers as well, on the contrary); the bookshops are still full of volumes by psychoanalysts written in alchemical language that means something only to those who have entered their temple, and perhaps not even to them. The exposure of Freud as a fraud, or a near-fraud, still comes as a shock in France, long after it has ceased to be such elsewhere in the western world. The question that remains, but that is not susceptible to a definitive answer, is why theories so arcane, so preposterously speculative, so lacking in evidence in their favour and even in the possibility of there being any such evidence, should for a number of decades have conquered the most scientifically-advanced regions of the world.

Anyway, the book was good knockabout fun for those, like me, who enjoy the demolition of easy targets; and the ad hominem, always the most enjoyable form of argumentation, is here permissible because Freudians resort to it almost at once in defence of themselves. He who argues by the ad hominem is refuted by the ad hominem; and which of us is not delighted to learn that Freud (or indeed any figure of great renown) was an unscrupulous money-grubber who had a long-lasting sexual affair with his sister-in-law. If only he had also poisoned his servants to prevent them from testifying to what they had seen, our cup would run over!

The importance of Freud in the cultural history of the West (but nowhere else, which should give at least pause to our tendency to self-congratulation) means that a book such as the one I was reading was not trivial, for all that it was flogging a moribund horse. But as soon as I entered the Memorial, with its wall engraved with the names of the 70,000 Jews deported from France to the camps during the war, vanishingly few of whom ever returned, one immediately feels that all subjects other than this—and the Gulag, Armenia, Cambodia, Rwanda, and perhaps Sendero Luminoso—are frivolous, without importance. Who cares whether or not psychoanalysis is founded upon scientific truths? This in turn is an absurd thought because the mind cannot reflect upon genocide alone; a world in which people thought and spoke only of the most important of subjects would be not only intolerable but filled with untruth.

The exhibition of the Hutu genocide of the Tutsi in Rwanda—to call it Rwandan without qualification raises all kinds of problems—was small but effective. I am not sure what exactly one learned from it, however, other than it is necessary always for prudent people to keep available to the mind the worst of which Mankind is capable, if not always present in it. No worst, there is none, wrote Gerard Manley Hopkins in another context, and, alas, the subsequent century was to prove him right. No worst, there is none: the pit is bottomless.

The texts accompanying the exhibits were not entirely satisfactory: but then perfection is not of this world. I found, for example, the strenuous denial of any physical differences whatsoever between the Tutsi and the Hutu, and the claim that the difference between the two groups was purely social in origin, not entirely convincing and in any case somewhat sinister in its implications. For it meant that, if there had indeed been genetic or physical differences between the groups, the genocide would have been in some way less serious, less abominable, than it was. But this is wrong: it matters, ethically, not a jot whether there was or was not a real biological difference between the Tutsi and the Hutu, or how great or small the genetic overlap between them is; for the simple fact is—it should hardly need pointing out—that it is wrong in any conceivable circumstances or for any reason whatever for people to massacre their neighbours in an attempt to wipe them out altogether: and this is so whether they are biologically indistinguishable or easily distinguished.

There was also a dog that did not bark in the exhibition: Burundi. That neighbouring country, very similar to Rwanda culturally and demographically (85 per cent Hutu, 14 per cent Tutsi, 1 per cent Twa), has been almost a mirror image to Rwanda. Burundi, unlike Rwanda, did not overthrow Tutsi political and administrative dominance at its independence from Belgium; and in 1972, after an uprising in which Hutu killed many Tutsi, up to 200,000 Hutu—equivalent to double that number in 1994, the year of the genocide in Rwanda—were massacred by Tutsi, including all those who had been to secondary school and who might therefore be supposed to represent a threat to Tutsi dominance. Whether or not this constituted genocide is unimportant: a massacre by any other name is just as terrible.

The genocide in Rwanda, long mooted and eventually planned

in full, took place in a context in which a predominantly Tutsi rebel movement was trying to overthrow the Hutu government in Rwanda (and soon afterwards succeeded, of course). It would be surprising if the example of what had happened in Burundi twenty years earlier under a Tutsi government had had no effect on the minds of the Hutu majority in Rwanda, though in fact the rebel movement planned no such conduct on reaching power. Shortly before the genocide, moreover, the first democratically elected Hutu president of Burundi Melchior Ndadaye, had been assassinated by Tutsi soldiers after only three months in office. The fact that the first president of Rwanda after the victory of the rebels would be a Hutu, as would be many of the ministers, was unsuspected at the time.

Why was Burundi not mentioned in the exhibition? It was not that the exhibition excluded historical context altogether: for example, much was made of the colonising power's strict division of the population into the racial categories of Hutu and Tutsi, much favouring the latter for educational and economic advancement. According to the exhibition's version, there was no real division between them before this, though as it happens the Mwamis, or Kings, of both Burundi and Rwanda were always Tutsi.

The reason that Burundi was not mentioned, I surmise, was that the organisers feared that explanation would slide into exculpation: that the fears of the Hutu, or rather those of many of the Hutu (for of course not all Hutu were alike), would justify the genocide, even if only in part, in the minds of visitors. The Belgian role in the creation of the situation could be mentioned because it was perfectly safe to blame them; but to mention the Burundian role would run the risk not only of blaming the victims but of exculpating the perpetrators: many people believing that understanding and forgiveness are one.

This is not so, of course. All human action takes place in an historical context, whether this context be on a large or a small scale. There are antecedents to every murder, and quite often the victim has behaved badly towards the perpetrator; but this in no way annuls the perpetrator's moral responsibility for his actions. It is true that there comes a point at which the conduct of the victim does excuse what would otherwise be a crime: self-defence, for example, is an absolute defence. But in the case of the Rwandan genocide, the people who were killed were not rebel soldiers seeking to overthrow the government, but peaceful neighbours and friends whose goods were coveted, stolen and enjoyed by the perpetrators in the most blatant possible fashion. In this instance, partial explanation is most definitely not exculpation, not even to a small extent.

Often we fear to explain human conduct, however, precisely because, try as we might to avoid it, explanation slides into exculpation. It is surely remarkable that so many books have been written about Rwanda that do not mention Burundi, except in passing as a destination for Rwandan refugees. This suggests either that the authors think that events in Burundi had no psychological effect upon Rwandan Hutu, or they fear that readers will excuse the inexcusable.

There was one further irony in the exhibition that went quite unremarked. It was that the Hutu government, before its overthrow, had a firm policy of positive discrimination, indeed it justified its existence in part by that very policy. Without this policy the Tutsi would have dominated education, administration and commerce, just as they did before the imposition of a *numerus clausus* in business, schools, universities, government offices, even in the Church (some of the upper clergy not only failed to condemn the genocide but actively encouraged it.)

The justification for the policy of positive discrimination in favour of the Hutu was that, without it, they would be underrepresented in positions of power, wealth and influence, an under-representation both unjust and undemocratic; and that it, the policy, was necessary to overcome the past discrimination against the Hutu that had reduced them to a chronically subservient position.

These arguments, unfortunately, are only too familiar in countries far away from Rwanda; they assume that, in a perfectly just society, where no one discriminates racially against anyone else, power, wealth and influence will be distributed in exact proportion to the weight of groups in the population. On this view, the decision of the Hutu government to limit the number of Tutsi students at the university to ten per cent (just below the proportion in the population) was perfectly reasonable and perhaps even obligatory. It redressed a balance in order to make society fairer.

I do not suppose that supporters of positive discrimination will care much for the analogy between what they propose and the policy of the last Hutu rulers of Rwanda, but it is there nonetheless. Naturally, the analogy is a strictly limited one, for not even the most fervent of positive discriminators outside Rwanda is in favour of genocide. Visitors to the United States who favour positive discrimination can therefore still answer truthfully the question on the entry form about whether they have ever committed or conspired to commit genocide. But what they cannot claim is to be is against racial discrimination—not that they are asked, yet.

15
Driven Mad

THE MOTOR CAR, a friend of mine once said, is the most liberating of all machines ever invented. Suffice it to say that I have not found it so, at least not in Europe, which is small and overcrowded and full of traffic jams. Once, for example, when I was going to visit my aunt, it took me two hours to go a hundred yards along the North End Road in London. I did not find it a liberating experience, unless the bringing to the surface of the inner demon that caused me to bang my fists on the windows in sheer frustration be counted as a liberating experience (for the inner demon, that is, not for me). I didn't know either that I had it in me to scream so loud. The only thing that calmed me down, other than embarrassment at being overheard, was the thought that the traffic jam would make a wonderful setting for a dystopian novel of the J. G. Ballard variety, illustrating the swift deterioration of human conduct, the almost immediate descent to barbarism, under the stress of a perpetual traffic jam. How long would it be before the people in the cars started to loot the shops along the side of the road in search of food, or attack one another in search of a bottle of water? Not very long, I would imagine, not more than a few hours, a day at most, so that the story would illustrate not just the fragility of civilisation but also the thinness of its veneer over the 'real' nature of Man. Why extreme situations should be considered more revelatory of our true nature than everyday ones is rather a mystery: perhaps it is to give us scope to descant on our own moral turpitude as a species, which is always a great pleasure.

Of course, not every car journey ends in a traffic jam, but still I do not find my own car liberating. Indeed, I almost find it imprisons me. I am reluctant to go anywhere in it because I have found such a good parking space in the road in which I live, a delightful street that goes all round a church and is to be reached only up a narrow lane between houses that date from the 15th to the 19th centuries.

The trouble is, of course, that there are almost as many cars owned by the inhabitants of the street as there adult inhabitants of it, which means a shortage of parking spaces. If I go out in my car, therefore, I cannot be sure to have a parking space on my return; and my street is the only place I am allowed to park as long as I like without charge (or should I say without *further* charge, for I had to buy my parking permit in the first place). If I don't park in my street, I have to park elsewhere—for a limited time only. Then I have to move the car again, or risk a fine. It is best, then, on the whole, not to go out in my car, to stay put in my house. It gives me less anxiety in the end.

Motor cars, like many other things such as mobile telephones, were all right when they were the perquisite of the few (and I didn't mind at all not being one of the few); but as soon as everyone got one, or in some cases more than one, the nightmare began. The roads clogged up, it took just as long to go anywhere as it had done before the arrival of the cars. The old Soviet joke begins to sound not quite as absurd as it might once have done.

> A political commissar is lecturing the troops about the differences between the United States and the Soviet Union when one of the recruits puts up his hand to ask a question.
>
> 'Is it true, Comrade Commissar,' he asks, 'that they in the United States have more cars than we in the Soviet Union?'
>
> The commissar thinks for a moment and then replies:
>
> 'Yes, comrade, but we in the Soviet Union have more parking spaces.'

Not quite so absurd in view of my reluctance to go anywhere in my car for fear of not being able to park on my return. I am thus a prisoner, if not of my car exactly, at least of my parking space; and I carry this anxiety around with me in a ridiculous fashion.

I spend quite a lot of time in Paris at the moment and usually I go by public transport, but sometimes I drive. The result is that when I see a parking space in the city, wherever it is, I think it a terrible pity I have not my car with me to take advantage of it. I regret it as a terrible missed opportunity; and this is so even if it is a street far from where I am actually staying. 'Suppose,' I think to myself, 'I were driving in this area and trying to park. Never in a hundred years would I find a space, and there is one going begging.' The thought depresses me, as if I had failed to make the most of my opportunities in life; I suppose my philosophy has become 'Gather ye parking spaces while ye may.'

So I am not really a fan of cars, I prefer public transport. I find it more relaxing as it relieves me from parking anxiety (not yet a diagnosis in the *Diagnostic and Statistical Manual of the American Psychiatric Association*, but surely destined one day to become one), besides which the human comedy on buses and trains is much to be preferred to the fruitless and frequently infuriated solipsism of driving. On a train, one can even sometimes read.

It was the absence of cars that makes me guiltily nostalgic for the communist days in Eastern Europe. You have only to compare Bucharest then with now to see what I mean. In good King Nicolae's day, traffic was very light and it was a delight, at least to me with my somewhat unusual tastes, to walk around the city, albeit that it was grey and dismal, its former grandeur decayed and its louche gaiety long since departed. It had its own atmosphere, one of slight menace, like the faint tingle that a small battery can impart to wet fingers. When in an empty street there was someone walking behind you, you assumed for a moment that he must be following you, a hypothesis to be tested by turning left or turning right even when you didn't need or want to. It was flattering, in a way, to think that you were worth following, or that anyone was sufficiently interested in you to bother with where you went, whom you met, and what you did, but of course surveillance was as much a matter of prevention and deterrence as of the detection of anything that you had done. Cars (as well as neon lights and any advertising other than political slogans) would have ruined the atmosphere and been completely out of place. The few vehicles that there were in the streets, though the owners of them were highly privileged by Romanian standards, were in a state of dilapidation, and exuded in gusts the smell of incompletely refined fuel, as well as little explosions of gritty black smoke; the buses, which trundled reluctantly and infrequently along the streets had great divers' tanks on their roofs, full of some kind of maximally-polluting gas that was probably distilled from tar and mangelwurzels.

I did not miss motor traffic at all. Visiting only briefly, it seemed to me that the slow pace among the big and once grand buildings was a kind of luxury, a wealth in time rather than in goods. It wasn't really any kind of wealth, of course; as Patrick McGuinness puts in in his wonderful fictional evocation of the end of the regime, *The Last Hundred Days*, 'it was surreal, or would have been if it wasn't the only reality available.'

When I returned to Bucharest a couple of years later, I could have sworn that the first fruit of freedom was traffic jams. Where had all those cars suddenly come from? They reminded me of the ants that appear on the counter of my kitchen in France if I leave a peach or some sugar on it. What were the ants doing before I did so? Surely they couldn't have just been waiting for my mistake? Anyway, it seemed to me that the choking traffic, now terrible, did not add to the charms of the city.

Tirana in Albania was even better, of course. It was said that there were only 500 cars in the whole country, so few in fact that you could be sure that if a car came up behind you there was a party bigwig in it. (Once, in Cameroun, I was on a bus going along a rutted laterite road when a fancy car swept by extremely fast, leaving a tsunami of dust behind. *'C'est un grand,'* said one of the passengers, a simple phrase that probably told you more about the running of the country than any number of books of political science.)

How wonderful was the peace of Tirana without cars! You could hear the faint murmur of conversation coming from the rickety apartment blocks so beloved of communist governments. You could walk in the middle of the widest boulevards with complete safety from traffic. On the other hand you and all your family could be sent down the mines for making a careless or mildly critical remark: there is no gain without loss.

People say in defence of cars that they allow people to go where they want, which is no doubt true. But in a small continent such as Europe, the very ease with which things may now be visited removes a great deal of the pleasure to be derived from visiting them. During the season, the south coast of France is more remarkable for its traffic than its natural beauty: it is easy to be stuck the whole day in a jam trying to get to the beach.

Cars *en masse* are ugly, and gone are the days (if only they would return) when you could have any colour you liked as long as it was back. These days, alas, people are allowed to express themselves by their choice of colour, and there are turquoise cars or bright yellow ones (all right in a pre-war Rolls-Royce, Bugatti or Hispano-Suiza, perhaps, but not in a little compact). A single bright ugly car can ruin an entire landscape, and often does so. Bright red is my *bête noire*, as it were, because, quite apart from its visual offensiveness drivers of such cars are inclined to like noise as well and to drive aggressively, as is reflected in the accident statistics.

A car is a millstone round one's neck. I have to pay a tax annually on mine, and woe betide me if I forget. I have to insure it and I have a strong suspicion that my insurance company is overcharging me, though I also resent the time and effort it would take me to find a cheaper policy. I also have to pay annually for my parking space, and each year the amount rises (last year by more than 300 per cent), and no lifetime subscriptions are available. A few passers-by scratch my car with keys for the sheer fun of it, which makes me, no doubt irrationally, detest the whole of the human race. And a car is a depreciating, though initially expensive, asset. There comes a time in one's life when one is afraid of depreciating assets, and I have reached it.

Not many people in the modern world refuse to learn to drive, but two things I have noticed about those I know who have done so: not only are they happier and more serene than their driving contemporaries, but they are usually superior to them in some way as well. This cannot be entirely a coincidence.

16
Fact and Tact

THERE ARE booksellers—quite a few, actually—who specialise in books about crime, both true and fictional. Among the categories they use is that of classic crime, a rather odd designation when you come to think of it: for when something is called classic it has a positive, even a laudatory, connotation, and crime, by definition, is something negative.

That a burglary, robbery, blackmail or murder should be good is against common sense and repellent to morality. Something can be good morally, aesthetically or functionally, but how could a crime be good in any of these respects? Yet we all know, more or less, what is meant by a classic crime: that is to say a crime with what Sherlock Holmes called points of interest, whether they be psychological, criminological, sociological, historical or forensic. Just as few books, or scientific papers, or works of art, rise to the status of the classic, so only a tiny minority of crimes achieve it. And we poor humans, most of us anyway, find the macabre fascinating, and fascination is an end in itself.

That, surely, was the point of De Quincey's essay—classic essay—on murder considered as one of the fine arts. Orwell more than a century later lamented the declining quality of murder, from the point of view of interest, in post-war Britain, and between these two great writers, Virginia Woolf's father—yes, Virginia Woolf's father—wrote an essay in 1869 titled *The Decay of Murder*, in which he too came to the conclusion that 'the style of the act is in a state of perceptible decline.' This was because 'Murders are [now] not only immoral—an objection to which they have long been liable—but they are becoming simply gross, stupid and brutal.' This was precisely Orwell's lament eighty years late.

'Murderers seem to me,' wrote Virginia Woolf's father Leslie Stephen, founder-editor of the *Dictionary of National Biography*, 'to be, for the most part, men of bad character and limited intelligence: and their patients are, as a rule, as stupid, if not as wicked, as the murderers themselves.' Stephen's judgment of murderers and the murdered is often, if by no means always, correct; and though Stephen was not notably a humorous man, the facetious use of the word patients (as well as the facetious style of the other passages I have quoted) suggests that murder as a subject brought out an elephantine irony in him, as it does in many writers (myself included). This is because, while murder is a dreadful act, and the closer one examines it the more dreadful it is both in itself and in its effects, it is difficult to find the precise tone in dealing with the phenomenon in general. If one adopts too solemn a tone, one appears to be labouring the obvious: that murder is bad, that people shouldn't commit it and that one is against it. Even the most cynical or mentally exhausted of hacks feels the need to write something not quite as obvious as that. After all, what need not be said needs not to be said; but, as the history of literature amply demonstrates, murder is a subject no writer can resist. One might even go so far as to say, no murder, no literature. A writer who is tired of murder is tired of writing; for there is in murder all the subject matter that life can afford.

Stephen had some shrewd things to say about murder as a subject of human interest, for example 'It is, of course, impossible to define the precise point at which the interest ceases to be legitimate, and testifies to a morbid state of mind rather than an excusable degree of sympathy with our fellow-creatures.' He is not among those intellectual puritans—or perhaps prigs would be a better word—who thinks that our attention should be directed towards objects in strict proportion to their importance as measured by some absolute standard of measurement, not only because such a standard might not be easy to find or prove, but because human beings are simply not constituted like that, and it would be horrible if they were. 'A ferocious monster enters a shop,' writes Stephen, 'knocks down all the inhabitants with a mallet, and cuts their throats with a razor. A few days later he repeats the performance with minor variations.' [This incidentally, is a description of the murder that inspired De Quincey. Note also the slight facetiousness of the word 'performance,' which has a distancing effect from the horror of what was done.]

'If,' continues Stephen, 'I am living within half-a-mile of the spot it is absurd to tell me that I should be too nice to listen to the details of the story...' And this is so even if, at the very time the murders were committed, an infinitely greater disaster, as judged by the total of suffering it caused, was taking place somewhere on the other side of the globe.

Of course, prurience can go too far: anything can. As a doctor I am not altogether sure that I liked Stephen's comparison of the prurient newspaper reader with doctors who read the *Lancet*:

> The spectacle [of the prurient reader of the newspaper] reminds us unpleasantly of doctors studying the *Lancet*, and leads us to fancy that our friends are merely searching for the latest news in the way of their profession. We fancy their motto to be, "We are murderers: nothing murderous is alien to us."

Why, I wonder, are so many literati hostile to doctors, when all they—we—want is the good of humanity? Traditionally, I have ascribed this hostility to either the failure of the literati to be admitted to medical school (as Hitler was rejected by the Art Academy of Vienna) or to resentment of the higher esteem in which doctors are held by the general public than that in which literati are held; but there is no record of Stephen ever having considered medicine as a career.

When it comes to murder, then, Stephen steers the middle course between prurience and priggery. I confess that the following words produced a stab of conscience in me when I read them, for reasons that I shall soon explain:

> Though we remember the extreme interest which all tourists display in seeing a place where some great man, of whom they never heard, performed some feat of which they are hearing for the first time, it must be admitted that local associations have a mysterious charm. When people take a step further, and deliberately go out for a picnic where a woman and her children were knocked on the head and buried in a ditch, I confess that they seem to me to show some moral obtuseness.

This discomfited me because, twenty years ago, I had myself been one of the morally obtuse tourists to whom Stephen referred. Shortly after one of the most notorious pair of serial killers in English history, Fred and Rosemary West, were arrested, I went to see their house as

Number 25, Cromwell Street, Gloucester, next door to a Seventh Day Adventist church. In that small house they had sexually tortured, murdered and buried nine victims, including their own oldest daughter Heather. I wanted to see the house before it was pulled down. Later, before his trial, Fred West committed suicide in the prison in which I worked as a doctor.

What, really, did or could I have hoped to learn by looking at the house? Was it not prurience pure and simple? The house itself was in a terrace of slightly run-down but perfectly habitable and even potentially elegant early Victorian houses, mostly divided into small flats. One imagined the social milieu in which the crimes took place—a shifting and even drifting population—but, without detailed research into the facts, such imaginings would remain purely speculative. A newspaper at the time, for example, interviewed a man who had lived in the road for more than twenty years, who said that West had seemed a good, ordinary person. If you cannot even discern the evil on such a scale by talking to the man himself, what purpose could there be to looking at the exterior of his house?

Yet, says Stephen, 'it must be admitted that local associations have a mysterious charm.' Charm, perhaps, is not quite the word for such an association in this case; but we all know the thrill, no doubt irrational, of handling a book or other object that was once in the possession of a great man. And in fact Gloucester City Council acknowledged the power of such irrational associations when it decreed the demolition of Number 25, Cromwell Street. If there were no power to such associations, why should it have done so? After all, the walls of a house are not responsible for what went on within them, nor is it very likely that, had the Wests lived elsewhere—at Number 19, for example—their conduct would have been much different. Yet no one protested that the demolition was absurd or even counter-productive (increasing, albeit imperceptibly, the housing shortage), and though I am not aware of any poll actually taken, I think it likely that the majority of the population of the city would have approved. Even if there is no spirit of a place, we continue to behave as if there were.

The houses of other notorious killers in England have also been demolished, for example 10 Rillington Place in London, where a man called Christie murdered eight women, and the whole street was reconfigured and renamed, the name indelibly sullied by association with Christie.

I happened to be in Gloucester nearly twenty years later for another purpose and, having half an hour on hand, I thought to revisit 25, Cromwell Street after its demolition. It is now a passageway to a parallel street, planted as a well-maintained garden, very much out of keeping with the rest of the area though no one who did not know the story would be able to guess why such an incongruous garden should be there. There is no memorial to the victims, nothing to indicate the appalling association of the place.

As I was looking at the garden, a man in what I should guess was a company car pulled up beside me. A man with a Manchester accent lowered the window and said, 'Excuse me, is that Fred West's house?'

He pointed to the Adventist Church, a miserable brick structure, and for a brief moment I considered telling him that it was, and that inside was a museum dedicated to the life and activities of Fred and Rosemary West which was free to the public. However, I thought better of it, and pointed instead to the garden.

'They knocked his house down,' I said. 'It was there.'

The man had been passing near Gloucester on his way back to Manchester from Bath on business, and he thought he would visit Number 25, as he called it, only a ten mile diversion from his direct route. It occurred to me that if you conducted a word-association test of British people who lived through the Fred and Rosemary West era (which lasted a few weeks, as eras nowadays do), and asked them for an association with the words Number 25, the majority would say 'Cromwell Street.'

My interlocutor, a salesman by trade, was an aficionado of murder, particularly of the serial variety. He first became interested in the subject after he was questioned by the police in connection with the activities of a man known as the Yorkshire Ripper, Peter Sutcliffe, who murdered at least 13 women, mostly prostitutes—not that he had any connection with the murderer's activities, he was only one of 11,000 people questioned by the police in their desperate search for the culprit. But by such accidents are our destinies affected—though not, of course, decided, for I am sure that not every person of the 11,000 of those questioned became aficionados of murder.

The correct tone in which to speak and write of past murder is difficult to catch. Prurience, solemnity, levity, censoriousness, disgust, outrage, indifference, irony, almost any attitude you care to think of seems wrong in one way or another. Here is the opening of an introduction to the trial of Adelaide Bartlett for having allegedly murdered her husband with chloroform: *There is a peculiar fascination about a case of poisoning.* This is not right, morally, one feels: and yet it is true.

17
Warmth is Cool

THERE ARE two types of men: those who divide men into two types of men, and those who don't. But just as there is an infinite number of ways of dividing a sphere into two, so (because of Man's infinite variety) there are an infinite number of ways of dividing men into two.

The other day, for reasons unnecessary to mention, I returned to Hume's essays. Hume was once a hero of mine because of the coolness and irony of his prose, the coolness of his thought and the coolness of his temperament. He was cool, not in the debased modern sense, but in the sense that the Stoics might have recommended and admired. I was attracted to him because by nature I was the opposite, hot-tempered and passionate. Temper and passion do not bring lasting happiness, and Hume exerted a lasting and I think beneficial effect on me.

In his first essay, *Of the Delicacy of Taste and Passion*, published in 1753, Hume divides humanity into two by two different criteria, related but not identical. Some people, he says, 'are subject to a certain delicacy of passion, which makes them extremely sensible to all the accidents of life, and gives them a lively joy upon every prosperous event, as well as a piercing grief when they meet with misfortune and adversity.'

We have all met people like that: for them there is nothing between triumph and catastrophe. Life in their eyes is ever a drama and minor incidents are for them indistinguishable from the Thirty Years' War or the discovery of America. Their emotions are to feeling what the primary colours are to a painters' palate.

People of this character, Hume says, 'have more lively enjoyments, as well as more pungent sorrows, than men of cool and sedate tempers.'

But Hume is in little doubt that the latter are, on the whole, more fortunate, on the somewhat pessimistic grounds that in human existence sorrows are more commonly met with than joys. He does not say actually say so, but the sum total of human happiness (the utilitarian measure of all things) would be greater if people were of more phlegmatic disposition.

Hume goes on to say that people differ in much the same way in their aesthetic reactions as in their emotional ones. Those who are quickly and peculiarly susceptible to beauty are likewise quickly and peculiarly pained by ugliness; while those who are indifferent to aesthetics enjoy neither the pleasures of beauty nor the pains of its opposite.

Does this mean that Hume thinks that an absence of aesthetic sensibility would be to the good or conduce to contentment? No, because though the two cases are analogous they are not the same, and he gives his reasons for saying so.

He says that, while we have little control over life in general, and that 'the good or ill accidents of life are very little at our disposal,' it is quite otherwise with matters of taste. We can, for example, choose the books we read and cultivate our taste. And this will cure us of any tendency that we might have to that exaggerated 'delicacy of passion' that he thinks so injurious to human happiness. For, he says, if we cultivate our taste 'we shall form juster notions of life [and] many things which please or afflict others, will appears to us too frivolous to engage our attention, and we shall lose by degrees that sensibility and delicacy of passion which is so incommodious.'

I am not sure that Hume is entirely right. It is true that we can arrange the aesthetics of our own tiny little corner of the world as we wish, provided that we have the time and means to do so, but we are as powerless over the aesthetics of the world in general as over the 'good or ill accidents of life,' and an excessive aesthetic sensibility, given the ugliness of the world, or much of what Man has done to the world (though he has also added to its beauty), will likewise pain us excessively. I think I am of that ilk: when I look at an otherwise beautiful landscape ruined by an excrescence, by no means an uncommon experience, I feel not pleasure at the beauty but pain at the ugliness. I cannot be grateful for the beauty and overlook the ugly. My sensibility is therefore too raw-nerved to go happily through the world and I sometimes envy those who are indifferent to what they see or hear. My problem is exactly that of those people who are 'extremely sensible to all the accidents of life;' I am ecstatic over the beautiful and crushed miserably by the ugly. And since one can hardly walk in this world of ours a step without seeing or hearing the ugly, it is an unfortunate excess of sensibility to have. It is only by the constant exertion of the will, the willing suspension of aesthetic judgment, that I avoid feeling crushed by ugliness all the time.

There is one field in which I think I have achieved the right balance of sensibility and indifference, and that is in gastronomy. I like very good food and will choose it in preference to bad, but at the same time I am fundamentally indifferent to it. Good food gives me pleasure, sometimes great pleasure, but not the kind of pleasure that I would find it hard to live without. If someone were to tell me that, for the rest of my life, I would have to live on stale cheese sandwiches, I should be a little sad, but I would soon make peace with the world. But if someone were to tell me that, for the rest of my life, I could listen only to rock music and read only airport novels, I should pray for a swift death.

Moreover, passion, not necessity, is the mother if not of all, then at least of most invention. People who achieve something in life usually overestimate the importance of what they are doing, and if they did not they would hardly achieve anything. There are, of course, overachieving dilettantes, but they are a minority of dilettantes and they are a minority of people who achieve something. Great poets think poetry the most important thing in the world, great entomologists, insects. At least in respect to their chosen fields, both are likely to be 'extremely sensible to all the accidents of life,' the poet, for example, elated by a good line and downcast to the point of despair by his inability to find the right word for what he wants to express. And of course it is that unhappiness that drives him on.

Clearly Hume would be more in favour of classicism than of romanticism, and on the whole I am with him there. But virtues, aesthetic as well as moral, turn into vices when pushed too far; classicism can become dry, formalistic, and deadening if it is permitted to go on for too long, while romanticism, called into being as a revolt against it, can become in time posturing, insincere and hectoring. Clearly there is a need for both, but what is the happy medium between them? Can it actually exist?

I once met someone who said that Alexander Pope was the greatest poet in the English language (once the habitual obeisance had been made to Shakespeare, of course). Now I am a great admirer of Pope both as a writer and as a man. There is no doubt that he was one of the wittiest persons who ever lived. His wit, if I may so put it, is deep: it infuses everything he does. It is not the wit of witticism alone; it is the wit of a world outlook.

It could be said that he wrote to a formula, a formula that he took from his times. But with what brilliance he used it! Here are the opening lines of *An Essay on Criticism*:

> 'Tis hard to say, if greater want of skill
> Appear in writing or in judging ill;
> But of the two, less dang'rous is th'offence
> To tire our patience, than mislead our sense.

When one considers that Pope was only twenty years old when he wrote this, one is astonished; for my part, I think that, after a lifetime of reading, I could rack my brains and not come up with anything half so good.

Nor were these four lines a luck hit: wherever you look, in *An Essay* or elsewhere in Pope, you find the same brilliance. Here are another four lines from *An Essay*:

> Of all the Causes which conspire to blind
> Man's erring judgment, and misguide the mind,
> What the weak head with strongest bias rules,
> Is Pride, the never-failing vice of fools.

Could you, reader, have thought, let alone written, anything like that when you were twenty? Can you now, indeed? Pope was a living example of his own dictum:

> True Wit is Nature to advantage dress'd
> What oft was thought, but ne'er so well express'd;
> Something whose truth convinced at sight we find,
> That gives us back the image of our mind.

When I wrote once of the brilliance of Doctor Johnson, I could think of no better way to put it than to say that he often said or wrote things that strike us immediately as simultaneously obvious and self-evident, and yet revelatory, and that this combination is joyful. But here was Pope, aged twenty, saying the same thing (not about Doctor Johnson, of course, but about wit in general), only better.

I open my Pope at random and anywhere find the same brilliance. Here are a few lines from *An Essay on Man*, in which never was a false philosophy expounded with so much aplomb. But it is not the falseness to which I draw attention, but the brilliance:

> Look next on Greatness; say where Greatness lies?
> 'Where but among the Heroes and the wise?'
> Heroes are much the same, the point's agreed,
> From Macedonia's madman to the Swede;
> The whole strange purpose of their lives, to find
> Or make, an enemy of all mankind!
> No one looks backward, onward still he goes,
> Yet ne'er looks forward further than his nose.

(The Macedonian, of course, was Alexander the Great, and the Swede Charles XII, whose constant warmongering ruined his country.)

Pope was not just a satirist, a good deal deeper than many give him credit for having been; his descriptions of nature were precise, the fruit of close observation (and no one observes closely what he neither values nor thinks important). Anyone who has lain in grass will recognise the aptness of this line:

> The green myriads in the peopled grass...

Nor was he devoid of feeling who could depict ageing beauties around a table thus:

> Beauties, like tyrants, old and friendless grown,
> Yet hate repose and dread to be alone...

But there is no denying that rhyming couplets, however coruscating their brilliance, their wit, their aptness, pall after a time, and give rise to a sensation almost of inhumanity. One senses how bad an example Pope would be for an imitator of lesser brilliance than he: a revolt against the Augustan manner was necessary, and one finds it in a romantic who could without absurdity be called the second greatest poet in English after Shakespeare, namely Keats. Surely the following lines are beyond the emotional power of Pope's rhyming couplets to convey:

> Darkling I listen: and, for many a time
> I have been half in love with easeful Death,
> Call'd him soft names in many a mused rhyme,

To take into the air my quiet breath;
Now more than ever seems it rich to die,
To cease upon the midnight with no pain…

Pope and Keats did share one thing: tuberculosis, Pope of the spine and Keats of the lung. Indeed, Pope's appalling health (for years he needed mechanical supports to stay upright, and not a day passed for him without pain and discomfort) called forth one piercing line from Pope that was no mere self-pitying exaggeration, and acted like a flash of lightning in a dark landscape:

The muse but serv'd to ease some friend, not Wife,
To help me thro' this long disease, my Life…

This long disease, my Life: who could ever forget these words, having read them?

In fact, we need both the coolness of classicism and warmth of romanticism, but they are not easily reconciled: which is yet one more reason why human life is not perfectible.

18
Flying High

JUST OVER twelve years ago, I was waiting outside a court to give my evidence in a case of murder. There was another expert witness outside waiting to give his evidence, too, and we fell to talking. I explained what I did, and asked him what he did.

'Oh,' he said of himself dismissively, 'I'm just a fly man.'

I am ashamed to say that until then I not only knew nothing of forensic entomology, I did not even know that such a subject existed. It had never occurred to me that the insect fauna found on a body might help to detect the perpetrator of a crime. Like so many ignorant people I had supposed that a maggot was a maggot, a repellent manifestation of Nature's malignity. My interlocutor enlightened me in a most charming and entertaining manner, though the subject was not one to please an aesthete.

In fact, he was a crucial witness in the case because much turned on the time of death of the victim and this could be estimated sufficiently accurately by the maggots and other insects that had been found on his body. This was not quite a straightforward matter, for the succession of insects that feed on a body depends on many factors, but once these are taken into account, the time of death can be established by such evidence with reasonable certainty.

All this was completely unknown to me—as unknown as the American continent was to Ferdinand and Isabella. It opened a fascinating and previously unsuspected vista to me; I could happily have listened to the forensic entomologist for hours. He had that happy knack of communicating his enthusiasm without being in the least overbearing or superior, or condescending because of the other person's—that is to say, my—ignorance. Though he had been in the field for many years, it had lost none of its wonder for him; he was proofed against cynicism.

Alas, he was called all too soon into court to give his evidence, which I did not hear, and I did not meet him again. But by coincidence, I received about two weeks later a letter from Dr Zakaria Erzinçlioğlu enthusiastically praising an article that I had written under my *nom de plume*. I realised at once that it was he whom I had met shortly before at the court, for he mentioned in the letter that he was a forensic entomologist (not a common profession), though he did not realise that he had met me.

I replied at once, thanking him for his flattering remarks, and told him that we had actually met shortly before. I hoped, in fact, that we might become friends, for I had seldom met so attractive a personality, expansive without egotism, an obvious enthusiast for the world about him. It was (I surmised) impossible to be in his company without learning a great deal.

I did not hear back from him and about a week later I opened my newspaper—to this day I love the sensation of opening a physical newspaper, a pleasure that no screen will ever give me—to see an obituary of him. He had died, aged 50, of a heart attack.

I was not only shocked but grieved by the news, so completely unexpected. To this day I cannot think of him—and I think of him surprisingly often—without a stab of grief.

Dr Erzinçlioğlu, known to his professional colleagues as Dr Zak, was a remarkable man. He was born in Hungary in 1952, and spent much of his childhood in the Sudan and Egypt. I thought it likely (though I do not know) that his parents were diplomats, and he was obviously of Turkish descent; at any rate he studied zoology in England and specialised in entomology. Apparently he became interested in the forensic aspects of his subject when one day the police came to him and asked him whether he could help in their investigations of a murder. From then on he did not look back.

He was on the verge of larger fame when he died, and I think he had the kind of personality that would not have been spoiled by it. He had published an entertaining book about his forensic cases, *Maggots, Murder and Men*, and had appeared on television. He was cultivated, with an interest in literature; he was an admirer of Sherlock Holmes and had published a short story in a collection of Holmes stories by contemporary writers. His first book was called *Blowflies*, a handbook of these generally despised insects (bluebottles and greenbottles among them) whose larvae live in carcasses.

Even in this short work he managed to communicate his enthusiasm for the subject. Can anyone not be intrigued by the information that blowflies of the genus Chrysomya in South Africa had been shown to fly distances of at least 63.5 kilometres? Or by learning that flies often land near a carcass before laying their eggs on or in it, perhaps as a means of avoiding predation?

I have had only two important experiences with blowflies in my life. Some blowflies—though none, fortunately, in Britain—are obligate parasites of living flesh, and in Africa I was once the victim of Cordylobia anthropophaga, the Tumbu fly. It was with horror but also fascination that I treated myself. The fly's larva, that does not need a pre-existing wound to burrow into human flesh, causes a swelling, but the larva can be forced to emerge from its burrow if its spiracle is covered by petroleum jelly so that it can no longer breathe, and this I did. From this I learned that a commitment to observation, even of oneself, can reduce, if not revulsion itself, at least the psychological consequences of revulsion.

Quite a lot earlier in my life, when I was still a child, I had found a toad, alive though clearly very debilitated, whose head was being eaten by maggots. Again I was repelled, and when later I told the adults what I had seen they refused to believe me. Such a thing could not be, they said. This taught me the necessity to hold fast to one's own direct experience and not accept that authority, *qua* authority, was always in the right. In Dr Erzinçlioğlu's book on blowflies, I discovered that I had been right all along and this is what I read therein:

> Lucilia bufonivora is an obligate parasite of toads (Bufo vulgaris) in Britain... The eggs are usually laid on the back or shoulders of the toad, and hatching is timed to coincide with the moulting of the toad, when there is a liquid exudate on the toad. The larvae invade the eyes and nostrils, killing the host and completing their development on the remains.

I was early cured of any tendency to nature mysticism by this toad and its parasites, or any illusion that nature was always kindly or beautiful. By contrast, it was always interesting, perhaps a more important quality.

As I have mentioned, I think of Dr Erzinçlioğlu surprisingly often, considering that I met him but once. But again as I have half-intimated, I have never met a man with whom I desired so quickly to become friends. And I must admit that I sometimes have unworthy and even dangerous thoughts about his death.

Why should so worthy a man, one who had so much to give the world, have died at so early an age when many lesser human beings, who consumed but did not contribute, survived for decades longer? It seemed unfair, even unjust. The universe should be better arranged.

I have to suppress these thoughts because, as the history of the Twentieth Century showed, that way madness lies. There is an existential equality to or inherent in Man—between men—that transcends their individual characteristics. This is recognised in medical ethics, according to which a doctor makes no enquiry into the moral worth of his patient, but treats him as best he can whatever he is like. When people discovered that I worked as a doctor in a prison, they asked me whether I did not find it difficult sometimes to treat people who had done the most terrible things. Oddly enough, I did not find it at all difficult; a doctor is like a lawyer at a trial who presents the best case he can on behalf of his client, even if he knows him to be a perfect swine. He puts such considerations out of his mind: it is not his place to decide whether a man merits his suffering, as in many cases he does; and what at first is a conscious decision soon becomes second nature. I once had a patient who, acting as a baby-sitter for a neighbour, impaled three children on railings, and who now had a cough. I treated the cough as I would have treated anyone else's cough. We are lucky to live in a society in which we do not treat people after their desert, for huge numbers of us are treated much better than we deserve.

By strange coincidence, Dr Erzinçlioğlu's little book quotes a definition of equality that brings to mind Hamlet's riposte to Claudius about how a king may go a progress through the guts of a beggar. According to the man who wrote this definition, the great self-taught French entomologist, Henri Fabre, the only meaning of equality is contained in the following:

> At the surface of the soil, exposed to the air, the hideous invasion [of maggots] is possible; ay, it is the invariable rule. For the melting down and remoulding of matter, man is no better, corpse for corpse, than the lowest of the brutes. Then the Fly exercises her rights and deals with us as she does with any ordinary animal refuse. Nature treats us with magnificent indifference in her great regenerating-factory: placed in

> her crucibles, animals and men, beggars and kings are one and all alike. There you have true equality, the only equality in this world of ours: equality in the presence of the maggot.

Hamlet, you may remember, tells Claudius that:

> A man may fish with the worm that hath eat of a king, and eat of the fish that hath fed of that worm.

When Claudius asks him what he means by this, Hamlet replies:

> Nothing but to show you how a king may go a progress through the guts of a beggar.

The worm of this passage, however, is a maggot; for while people may fish with an earthworm, earthworms do not eat of human bodies, but maggots, known also at the time as worms, do. And although it was proved only in 1668 (by a Florentine physician, Francesco Redi) that maggots were not spontaneously generated in rotting flesh, as many at the time supposed, but were the product of eggs laid by flies, Shakespeare knew perfectly well that flies generated maggots. So Shakespeare agreed with Fabre, that maggots and flies taught Man a lesson in existential or transcendental equality.

So I try to put thoughts of the unfairness, the injustice, of Dr Erzinçlioğlu's early death out of my mind. A life is not well-lived, in any case, according to its length. We are not far off the time when almost everyone will live three times as long as Schubert, but no one will conclude that each life will then be three times as well-lived as was his. Still, I should not be telling the truth if I did not admit that thoughts, which are both dangerous and absurd, recur to me, and which I have to struggle to dismiss from my mind, that it would have been better if someone could have died in Dr Erzinçlioğlu's place.

It is strange, though, how such absurd and dangerous thoughts return to torment us (or at least me). When my much-beloved little dog was still alive, I used to wonder whether, if it were a choice between his life and that of a human being, which I would choose to save. Guiltily I had to acknowledge that I would prefer to save the life of my dog, though in practice I might act otherwise. And then there is the stupid but recurring question, if you could have only the work of one artist, one writer, one composer, which would it be? Fortunately, we are never called upon to answer these question, so why do we ask them?

19
Chinese Puzzles

ONE PICTURE, said Mao Tse-Tung, is worth a thousand words, and in a sense he was right. A thousand words cannot describe adequately your current visual field, or even the tiniest part of it (I don't think you should even try); but neither can pictures adequately convey what you are able to say in words. We don't have different faculties for nothing.

I used rather to despise books that consisted mainly of pictures, but recently I have changed my opinion. (Even what I consider to be recent has changed with age, ten or even fifteen years ago now seeming to me quite recent). I don't go as far as Alice, who doubted the use of books without pictures; but neither do I any longer doubt the use of books without words, or almost without words. Perhaps childhood and second childhood are the ages at which one appreciates pictures in books.

It is possible that my new-found appreciation of picture-books is a sign of cognitive decline: that I no longer have the patience, concentration or memory to read great blocks of print (perhaps the young never will, thanks to electronic screens of all kinds). But I do not think so, I still regularly read tomes that others might consider intimidating in density and length. There is also the possibility that I have changed my mind simply to prove to myself that I am still capable of doing so, that I do not suffer from that condition that a brilliant friend of mine called the hardening of the concepts, worse even that hardening of the arteries (though sometimes associated with it). But again I do not think so. Rather it is that, thanks to the passage of time, my memory is now so well-stocked that images easily evoke the recollections or associations that are the principal consolation of one's declining years. This is also one of the pleasures of browsing in second-hand bookshops: a recollection or association evoked by chance is more pleasurable than one that is systematically search for.

Last week I came across (and bought, despite its extravagant price) a book of photos titled *L'Empire Céleste,* the Celestial Empire. As this would suggest, it was a book about Imperial China, though in fact there were also pictures in it of the republican period up to the 1930s.

My connections to and with China are few and tenuous. I have been twice to the country; the first time convinced me that China's industrial pollution is a serious problem (and that was only at the beginning of China's dramatic economic growth!), and the second time was to report from Peking for a newspaper on a giant United Nations jamboree there on the condition of women in the world. At the press conference given by a British minister, who in her brief preliminary statement demanded that the health of men and women be equalised, I asked whether this meant that men should live longer or women should live shorter. A British civil servant stepped forward like an adult protecting a child (the minister) and said that my question was not serious and therefore unworthy of an answer: an answer that the minister in any case could not have given because she had by then grown so accustomed to the sound of her own platitudes. For myself, I thought that my question went straight to the heart of egalitarian philosophy, but that of course was its problem.

When I was a child my father had a multi-volume pictorial history of the war (it was called *Hutchinson's Pictorial History of the War*, and I still recall its heavy green embossed covers). I spent many hours looking at it, but the one photo that affected me most was of China. It was of a dead baby in a flimsy makeshift coffin in a field of rubble with ruins in the background, and no other human in sight. I must have been less than eleven years old at the time, for we moved when I was eleven and the books did not come with us. That one picture more than any other gave me an early appreciation of the horror of war, though like any other boy at the time I enjoyed making models of the aeroplanes that helped to bring it about.

My maternal grandparents were refugees in Shanghai, but they died at the end of the war and are (I believe) buried there. I was surprised to discover after my mother's death that she had received letters in England from them throughout the war, presumably through the good offices of the Red Cross. One of the letters to her from her father in Shanghai said, 'It is a beautiful spring morning and the sun is shining brightly, but there is no sun bright enough to penetrate the dark clouds that are covering the whole earth.' He went on to express the belief that one day the clouds would clear, but his hope was clearly less strong and more hypothetical than his despair, the reasons for which were all too real and evident. He died at just about the time the clouds were clearing, in 1945, but had he remained in China he soon would have seen them gather again.

There are a few photographs in the book of Shanghai as he would have known it, but of how he lived, in what conditions, I have no knowledge. My mother's sister, who was also a refugee in Shanghai and learned good Chinese, never wanted to talk about her past and it did not seem right to badger her into doing so. As the ancient Confucian sage, Xun Zi, put it, to talk *à propos* is a sign of knowledge, but so is to remain silent *à propos*. Now that she has died I shall never know, and can only surmise.

The photographs taken at about the time of my grandfather's arrival in the city do not make it look desperately poor, at least not by the standards of, say, the Calcutta of the same period. No one is wearing rags, everyone looks purposeful and busy. It is true that the wheeled traffic is shared between smart cars and rickshaws, and the pulling of rickshaws have always seemed to me the acme of human indignity, one man straining all his usually cord-like muscles to pull another man sitting back in comfort; but there is certainly no atmosphere of desperation in the pictures.

Did the camera lie? Not in the sense that it produced an image of what was not there to be seen, or in the sense that something had been airbrushed out in Stalinist fashion. But of course no number of photographs could capture the whole of reality, and everyone who wields a camera has a point of view, something that he wants to convey to others, and many things that he does not want to convey to others. Even the framing of a photograph for purely aesthetic reasons excludes what disturbs a composition, an ugly building next to a beautiful one, for instance. The camera is susceptible to all the rhetorical tricks of speech.

One's ideas can be upset or overturned by a photograph, both for good and harm. In this book, for example, there is a double page picture of opium smokers in a Hong Kong opium den of the 1890s. In the picture, five men, all of them young except for one, take their ease in a décor that is the Chinese equivalent of Victorian clutter. They are clearly men of refinement, and one young man looks severely intellectual, with round spectacles and a faraway look, as if imagining the answer to some deep scientific question. The scene is the very opposite of the degradation one immediately associates with the term opium den, and one is morally certain that the men in the picture, who are probably of the merchant class, are by no means rendered incapable of normal life by their facultative resort to the drug, no more than a man who drinks in a bar must be rendered incapable thereby of meeting the demands of normal life.

In his wonderful book about China titled *On a Chinese Screen*, published in 1922, that consists of many short and brilliantly economical chapters of description, Somerset Maugham extols an opium den that he visits as being much more civilised than the average bar or pub in England. What does this tell us, apart from that our prejudices might be wrong? It raises at least the possibility that opium smoking in China was not as nationally debilitating as is usually claimed, and indeed there is one modern school of Chinese that claims precisely this. The question cannot be answered, however, merely by looking at one picture or by reading one verbal sketch by Somerset Maugham: the photographer or Somerset Maugham may have found the one opium den that was not sordid as, for example, the opium den described by Dickens at the beginning of his last novel, *The Mystery of Edwin Drood*, is sordid.

Another layer that obtrudes between the photographs and the direct apprehension of the reality of which it is all too easy to suppose that they must be a representation is the choice among all possible photographs of China made by the editors of the book. Because of that choice, one might suppose, for instance, that public execution played a large part in Chinese life about the turn of the century (the nineteenth to the twentieth, that is), a supposition that could be either right or wrong.

The most startling of these photographs is of a public execution in Peking in 1908. A man is held down with his arms behind his back by two others kneeling beside him, the executioner bringing down a sharp sword on his neck with an intense chopping motion. In the foreground are the decapitated corpses of two men already executed, their heads removed, blood from the stumps of their necks soaking into the ground. The neatness of the severance gives some idea of the sharpness of the sword used by the executioner.

The executions seem to be taking place in a very informal fashion. The crowd of spectators, including three European soldiers (one of them a sergeant), looks on with intense interest, and very close up, almost cramping the style, if I may so put it, of the executioner himself. There is nothing like a beheading, it seems, to draw a crowd, and one suspects that the executioner takes a pride in, and even enjoys, his work. The

Moslem beheaders of western hostages are only too aware of the pleasures of decapitation, both for a prurient audience and for the sadistic performer. Man is not so much a wolf to man as the executioner of man.

Another photograph taken at about the same time is of men being slowly strangled to death by a strange apparatus consisting of a wooden cage inclining at an angle, in which they are suspended by a wooden halter which lifts them above the ground until they suffocate. There are four such apparatuses in view, but only two in current use. In the background, life goes on as if nothing unusual were taking place: which perhaps it wasn't.

There are other photos of condemned men, in one case of a boy with a chain round his neck connected to a heavy stone, presumably to prevent his escape. And we see also two accused men arriving in court to be questioned: they crawl on the ground, unable to stand because of heavy wooden halters around their necks.

Were these photos taken to prove to a western audience how savage were the Chinese and how much in need supposedly of a western civilising mission? Perhaps. But there are also many photographs that prove the exquisite refinement of Chinese civilisation. It is false, wishful thinking that is, however, often expressed in the hope that repetition will make it true, that civilisation is indivisible, that in all respects (art, architecture, the treatment of prisoners) it marches in unison ever forward and upward, as if it were a North Korean parade. We should never succumb to the complacent idea that because we are advanced in some respect or other we are therefore incapable of barbarism, or that because our telephones work so well our art or architecture must be similarly advanced.

20
And Death Shall Have His Dominion

THERE ARE many ways of dividing humanity into two other than those who divide humanity into two and those who don't. For example, there are those who are attracted to cemeteries and those who are repelled by them. I am of the former moiety: cemeteries are for me like bookshops; I find it difficult to resist the temptation to enter them and linger awhile.

I have been like this ever since my adolescence and I do not think I am morbid. On the contrary, I find it strange that some hurry past cemeteries either without a second look or even with a shudder. Meditation on the transience of life, intermittent rather than continuous and rejuvenating rather than paralysing, is important for achieving equanimity. And there is no better aid to such meditation, I find, than a good graveyard.

When I am in Paris I stay within a stone's throw of Père-Lachaise, perhaps the most famous cemetery in the world. Certainly it has more very celebrated people buried in it than any other cemetery that I know: you turn a corner and there is Balzac, with Delacroix not very far away. Most visitors go in search of the buried eminent, and indeed I have a guide that will take you straight to them, though I never use it. I prefer the tombs of the never-heard-of, but also of the once-heard-of-but-now-forgotten. They seem to me a greater stimulus to the imagination than the tombs of those everyone has heard of; and it seems almost a cliché to make straight for Oscar Wilde, as so many visitors do, who is perhaps the most famous inhabitant of the cemetery. The fact is that Sir Jacob Epstein's tomb is an aesthetic abomination, his most famous and at the same time his worst work. My guide, which is French, delights to point out that an Englishwoman, outraged by the sight of the carved figure's genitals, destroyed them with a hammer, thus confirming the French view of the English as a nation of hypocritical and unsophisticated prudes and puritans. The tomb is now protected by screens of what looks like bullet-proof glass, a case of closing the stable door after (if I may be allowed a mixed metaphor) the prude has hammered. It, the glass, is smothered in the red lipstick of those who have kissed it, and the last time I walked past someone had managed to insinuate one of those shiny plastic Chinese teddy-bears with a mechanical waving arm (in this case the battery had run out and the arm waved no longer), of the kind that one sometimes finds at the entrance to cheaper Chinese restaurants, into the space between the tomb and its protective glass. This led me to the melancholy reflection that prudes are probably preferable to sentimentalists, though perhaps not by a wide margin.

I prefer to wander at random among the 65,000 graves than seek out anyone in particular. When I was a child, the advertising slogan of the vulgar British Sunday newspaper, the *News of the World* (though of course it was not in those days nearly as vulgar as it was to become under the ownership of Mr Murdoch) was 'All human life is there,' and the same might be said, figuratively speaking, of Père-Lachaise. So inexhaustible is it, the cemetery I mean, that it would almost be a pleasure to reside there permanently were it not for the rather stringent residence qualifications. At the least it must be some slight consolation for the dying to know that they are to be buried there.

Although I do not seek out the famous, it is pleasant to stumble across them from time to time. For example I went inland, as it were, from a tomb adjacent to one of the main intersecting thoroughfares of the cemetery, the tomb of 'our dear son, Albert Rapilly, lieutenant, 1893–1918, Died on the field of honour, 29 July, 1918.' This tomb had a metal bas-relief, of the young man in his uniform, killed only three months before the end of the war. The simple inscription still conveys the pain of the parents, more eloquently indeed than a more florid one would have done.

A couple of tombs behind that of Rapilly I chanced upon that of Marcel Proust, a simple black stone slab with his name and dates of birth and death, and a Maltese cross. There were a few single roses lying across it and a torn-out page of a notebook, looking somewhat bedraggled as it had rained not long before. I picked up the paper out of curiosity to know what the person had written. It was in Spanish, but I couldn't make out the name:

> Thank you for having opened new horizons to me, for having made me see that everything in life, everything, everything, everything, is literature.

Was the writer of this himself an aspiring, or perhaps even a successful, writer? The pedant in me protested that not everything in life is literature: rather everything in life is potentially the subject of literature, which is not quite the same thing. Or was such literal-mindedness to destroy the poetry of what Proust's admirer had written, I think with real sincerity?

Père-Lachaise, perhaps any cemetery, is an antidote to pride and self-importance. There was a vogue for a time in Paris, between about 1870 and 1900, for metal busts of the deceased to be placed atop the columns or obelisks of their tombs. Naturally, these people were of some prominence in their time, for such funerary monuments could not have been cheap, nor could they have been mass-produced. They are now covered in verdigris, and personally I find them rather splendid, though they also make me smile. In general the men—they are always men—commemorated in this way look like good Victorians, at least with flourishing moustaches or mutton-chop whiskers. They were evidently important in their time, Laurent Monnet, for example, *Négotiant*, merchant, who died in his 50s, strangled (as it seems) by his shirt collar that wasn't large enough for his bon-vivant double chin. Though a resident of Paris, he died in Vichy in 1899, one imagines of a heart attack after or even during a too-copious and self-indulgent dinner of the kind in which he indulged just once too often. Monnet was almost certainly a prominent man in his time, or at least in his circle, but he is now at one with Nineveh and Tyre (as we shall all soon be ourselves): or, to change the poetic metaphor, the paths of profit lead but to the grave.

Père-Lachaise is, as everyone knows, the last resting-place of many men (fewer women) of world fame: but for every such person there are ten, twenty, foot-soldiers in the armies of achievement. They too were prominent in their day, but are now forgotten, except perhaps by super-specialists. The verdigris-busted tombs are often those of artists, *Chevaliers* or even *Officiers* of the *Légion d'Honneur*, directors or administrators of the École des Beaux-Arts, though the only thing that should matter for an artist's reputation, his art, is now forgotten. Jean-Joseph Weerts (1846–1927), for example, is there, an academic painter of Belgian origin who was clearly a man of considerable ability and yet whose pictures now horrify us by their kitschiness, their literal realism but emotional preposterousness, in short their bad taste. Was it Weerts' fault that, despite his gifts and technical accomplishments, he painted so badly? If he had been born, for example, in the Dutch Golden Age (whose very sudden decline, within the space of a few years only, seems to me a puzzle of art history), he would no doubt have earned himself an honourable, if minor, niche in history as, say, a painter of herrings on pewter plates, or of bouquets of flowers with symbolic insects, caterpillars, moths etc. He had not the penetration to see, though gifted in other ways. Since one may suppose that raw artistic ability is distributed evenly throughout the ages, taste becomes a distinguishing feature of the great artist. But taste is a collective as well as an individual matter, and it was easier to become a good artist in seventeenth century Delft or Haarlem than in twenty-first century Akron or Limoges.

There are many unheard-of scribblers as well in Père-Lachaise, at least unheard of by me. Almost every time I enter the cemetery I pass the tomb of Vertanes Assadourian (1907–2000), an Armenian writer who used the name Serovpe Mkhitarion. He was born in Van, in Ottoman Turkey, and (I surmise) escaped the genocide in 1915. But his writings, whatever they were, have left little trace: I have found only a book published in 1968 in Paris, in Spanish, by him, with the title *The Armenian Question*. How arbitrary are, or can be, our destinies: to be born in such a place at such a time!

You could walk through Père-Lachaise and find a thread of political torment running through it—if you so wished. Near the entrance which I always use is a double tomb, that of Jeanne and Monique Lacraze, aged 74 and 3 respectively, 'victims of the bombing [of Paris] on 13 August, 1944.' Very near to theirs is the tomb of Ebrahim Zaker, '*Modjehad du people et héro de la résistance iranienne*,' though without making it quite clear to the layman such as I who or what the deceased had resisted, the Shah, the Ayatollah or both: there is always so much to resist.

And not far is the tomb of Mahmoud Al Hamchari, born in Um Khaled, Palestine, on 29 August 1939, killed in Paris 9 February 1973 while 'representing the PLO.' He was blown up by an Israeli bomb in his Parisian flat: the Israelis believed he was the head of Black September in France and had participated in the planning of the attack on the Israeli athletes at the Munich Olympics.

One of the more curious political tombs is that of Masih Rasti Mobarake (1946–2004). 'Communism,' says the inscription, 'is humanity's resurrection,' a rather curious choice of words for militant atheists, when you come to think of it.

Below his is inscribed the name of Azar Derakhshan (1959–2012), without any explanation of the connection, if any other than political, of the two. Derakhhshan left 'luminous traces on the shore of life' (I don't think this is meant as damnation with faint praise), and she was 'a combatant communist and militant of the women's movement.' An Iranian refugee in France, she was a member of the anti-lapidation committee: a good cause, though I did briefly wonder, with shamefaced irreverence, whether there existed a pro-lapidation committee, and whether indeed it existence would be permitted.

It seems that communist opinions are almost an hereditary condition, for on the tomb was also a ceramicised photograph of an old lady, Mahmonir Sanjari (1923–2003), taken, I should guess, when she was in her late sixties, with a hammer and sickle in the background, probably at some dismal meeting in a cold, unheated, obscure hall somewhere, possibly in the suburbs of Paris, where all the participants believed that, notwithstanding the evidence to the contrary, they were constructing a glorious future. She might have been the matriarch of the others on the tomb (there were two others): or maybe it is just that birds of a feather are buried together. Much as I do not admire the political choices of these people, and believe that if they had been successful in their plans they would have instituted a different kind of tyranny, I could not help but find something noble in their devotion to what they thought would bring freedom and happiness. There is nobility in failure, especially when it persists for a lifetime; and as individuals I would probably have found these people much more congenial than many successful persons with whose views I agree.

But most of the tombs in Père-Lachaise, as in every other cemetery, are of people who led ordinary lives. I liked the words of the wife of Émile Huron (1883–1949) inscribed on his tomb, not orthodox but surely deeply felt:

Your memory is my religion.
This tomb is my homeland.
You… my love.

21
A Battle of Algiers

WHEN ASKED about the effects of the French Revolution, the late Chou En-Lai, as charming and sophisticated as he was without scruple, is alleged to have said, 'It is too soon to tell.' He probably never said it, however, which is rather a pity because it is so witty and, in a sense, true. The effects of any historical event stretch indefinitely into the future and therefore achieve no finality, which is why history constantly requires and undergoes revision even without the need of a totalitarian dictator, such as Stalin or Mao, to write people into or out of it according to the latest pattern of favour and disfavour. History will come to an end only with the extinction of the human race, and not with the triumph everywhere of liberal democracy, or of anything else for that matter.

Nevertheless, some episodes of history weigh more heavily on the present than others, and among the history that still weighs very heavily indeed in the present world, on both sides of the Mediterranean, is the Algerian war of 1954 to 1962. The French would rather forget that practically an entire generation of its men, born between 1932 and 1943, was sent to Algeria to fight to keep it French, often using the most brutal methods; the Algerians (or at least the Algerian government) would rather forget that not only did its side in the war commit many atrocities, both against the French colonists of Algeria and tens of thousands of Algerians, but that the Algerian population had not been unanimously supportive of the FLN before the advent of independence.

Nowhere has the whirligig of time brought in its revenges with a more acute sense of irony than in this case. The first fruit of a war fought in the name of a struggle against racial injustice and discrimination was *de facto* ethnic cleansing, that is to say of the million French residents of Algeria, 11 per cent of the population, including Jews, practically all of whom left Algeria in the few months after the signing of the Evian Accords in 1962. And, as the subsequent history of the country has proved, the so-called freedom fighters turned out to have been fighting not so much for freedom as for power. They were power-fighters rather than freedom-fighters, for once they were installed in power they instituted nothing that any political philosopher would recognise as a regime of freedom. The only sense in which the new regime was freer than the old had been was freedom from the old oppressor. The new oppressor (who immediately killed 15-30 thousand of his fellow countrymen who had fought on the old oppressor's side) was, however, of the same ethnic, cultural and religious origin as the population it oppressed. How much of an advance was this, and was it worth the lives of half a million people to make it?

If the answer is yes, then it is to admit that it is preferable to be oppressed by one's own people rather than by people of alien origin, even if the weight of the oppression is 'objectively' similar. But if that is so, it is to admit that racial, religious and cultural identity are morally important in politics, precisely what so many people would like to deny because it is so uncomfortable to have to admit it, and can so easily unleash the vilest political passions. Something that is true, say our people of goodwill to themselves, could have nasty consequences; therefore it is not true.

Back to the question, is it better to be oppressed by people of the same racial, religious and cultural identity as oneself than to be oppressed by aliens? There is something to be said on both sides. To be oppressed by a foreigner gives an extra dimension of outrage to the oppression, but on the other hand permits the hope that if only the foreigner can be expelled all will be well; to be oppressed by one's own countryman avoids the extra dimension of outrage, but does not permit of the comforting illusion of a simple solution. On the contrary, it suggests that there is something flawed in one's own traditions, which leads either to despair or to the espousal of ludicrous utopian schemes of political salvation or redemption.

Another of the ironies of the Algerian war is that its conclusion almost certainly benefited the French population as a whole more than the Algerian population as a whole. Indeed, it saved France without saving Algeria. Had Algeria remained French, full rights as French citizens would almost certainly have had to be granted to Algerians, including the right to live in Metropolitan France. They were 9 million at the time of independence fifty years ago, but they are 39 million now; and whatever problems France may now have with its population of North African origin, they are tiny by comparison with what they might have been if there had been absolutely free movement between the countries.

When President Chirac visited Algeria, he was greeted by crowds of young men chanting 'Visas! Visas!' Nationalist indoctrination and propaganda had not blinded them to their own personal interests, which was to find work in ex-colonial France (I very much doubt, contrary to what some demagogues say, that they dreamed of a life on social security.) Meanwhile, in France, young men of Algerian descent express contempt and even hatred for their country of adoption, for example by booing and whistling at the national anthem in a stadium when France play Algeria at a football match. (Admittedly, the Marseillaise has the bloodthirstiest and most morally reprehensible lyrics of all national anthems, including the wish that our furrows may be swamped by the impure blood of our ferocious aristocratic enemies. But these were not the grounds on which the Marseillaise was shown such disrespect, a disrespect that caused considerable anxiety in France.)

Recently I read—and looked at—an illustrated history of the Algerian war by Benjamin Stora, one of the most lucid and readable historians of the war and its continuing effects. He grew up with the war, as it were, having been born in Algeria in 1950; he left his native land with his parents in 1962. His mother, who spoke to him partially in Arabic, never accustomed herself to the impersonality of life in suburban Paris.

Stora seems genuinely even-handed in his treatment of the war, which the French won militarily but lost politically (happily for them). He extenuates no one and does not excuse the atrocities of anyone, including those of the FLN—though he suggests that the French army's use of torture during the Battle of Algiers, when it took control of the city from the infiltrating guerrillas of the FLN, may have been militarily useful, an uncomfortable conclusion for those who would like to believe that torture is not only morally wrong but useless in practice.

To only one person does Stora show himself unduly indulgent: François Mitterand, the former, and late, president of France. Mitterand was Minister of Justice during much of the most violent phase of the war. In that time he confirmed the death sentences of four out of five of the many Algerian rebels who were sentenced to death by courts (most deaths, of course, were extra-judicial). Many hundreds of people were executed when he had the power to stay the executions; but it was under his presidency, in 1981, that the death penalty was finally abolished in France.

Stora wonders how Mitterand could have undergone such a change. I do not think there is any real need to wonder, or to waste much time on such wondering. Mitterand did not so much change his mind—not like General de Bollardière, who resigned his post rather than continue to serve while torture was being carried out on a large scale by his men—as see on which side his political bread was buttered. By 1981 it was politically more profitable to him to be an abolitionist, just as in 1956 it had been politically more profitable for him to have been a willing executioner. Neither truth nor morality ever meant much to Mitterand in his pursuit of power, and even in a profession remarkable for its cynicism he stood out as outstandingly lacking in principle. I suspect that he thought that principles were strictly for the naïve.

Two photographs in Stora's book particularly affected me. One was of the beach near Algiers taken in April, 1962. There are sunbathers in bikinis on it, as if nothing unusual were happening. True, the placard behind them advertising Coca-Cola ('refreshing') was scrawled with graffiti in support of the O.A.S., the Secret Army Organisation, a dissident branch of the French Army opposed to General De Gaulle's policy that was then carrying on terrorism of its own on quite a large scale; but clearly for some, the state of their tan was more important than that of the country.

Was this stupidity or *sangfroid* on a magnificent scale? Within weeks those sunbathers would be refugees in France, probably deprived of all that they owned. But perhaps they simply accepted that they were in a hopeless and powerless situation, as eventually we all are, and therefore that they might as well continue with their normal pleasures. They would thus have one day more of sensual pleasure than if they sat lamenting: sufficient unto the day being the evil thereof. By sunbathing they were taking seriously at least one of the injunctions in the Sermon on the Mount.

The other photograph showed a gravely injured woman, Mme Monnerot, being lifted on a stretcher from a helicopter towards an ambulance, on November 1, 1954. That was the date on which the nationalist movement in effect declared war on the colonial regime, suddenly carrying out thirty simultaneous explosions in Algeria, its existence as an armed force having previously been unsuspected. (Mme Monnerot's husband, a teacher, who was killed in the explosion that injured her, the first fatality of the war.)

The photograph reminded me of my time in Rhodesia, as it then was (Zimbabwe now). There were two hospitals in the city of Bulawayo at the time, one for blacks and one for whites and the very few blacks who could afford to be treated there. (The treatment in both was of a very high standard.)

A friend of mine, a doctor, had a house in the grounds of the hospital for whites and I happened to be visiting when the first casualty of what was soon to be the guerrilla war arrived by helicopter. Until then security had seemed to be absolute but, young as I was, I knew this to be an historic moment, and that Rhodesia would not long survive as Rhodesia. Most of the Rhodesians, however, did not take the sign very seriously, indeed they took it almost lightly, as if the whole thing were an amusing distraction rather than a harbinger of a complete change. How could they be so blind to the obvious? The answer is clear: we can blind ourselves to anything we do not want to see. The writing on the wall is always written in ink that is invisible to someone or other.

Moreover, there is none of us who has never failed to see some or other writing on the wall. Our clairvoyance, if we possess any at all, is always limited both in time and place. However clear-sighted we are about some things, we are always blind about others. And as if wilful blindness were not enough, there is the inherent unpredictability of things. We imagine that a corollary of free will and the absence of fatality means that can control the future, but this does not follow at all. The glass through which we see things is always dark.

Yet if foresight is impossible, it is also necessary. I do not find this depressing, on the contrary I am thankful for it. How dull an existence it would be if all that were necessary were also possible!

22
Of Chekhov, Dickens, Henley and Pascal

CHEKHOV SAYS somewhere that a writer should be able to write a story about an ashtray. Although I have not tried the experiment, I think he is right and in fact it would not be all that difficult to do so. If ashtrays could speak, what tales they could tell! Many have been flung in anger in the course of an argument, but even without such violent drama they would practically all have witnessed (if they had been capable of witnessing) untold emotional crises. Cigarettes are, after all, for many the emotional prop of first and last resort, the heart of a heartless world, to adapt slightly Marx's dictum about religion. They are not the opium, but the nicotine of the people.

Inspiration, then, should be everywhere, if only we exercised our curiosity and imagination sufficiently. For example, the other day I had occasion to visit the elegant house of an old literary couple. They were obliged by circumstances to leave me alone for a time in their drawing room-cum-library, and I amused myself (at their suggestion, but I would have done it anyway) with their books. I took down the eighth volume of the magnificent Pilgrim edition of Dickens' letters, Dickens being a man of such prodigious genius that his every sentence even on the most banal of subjects sparkles. He called himself the Inimitable, and that is what he was.

The volume fell open between pages 290 and 291, and my eye alighted on a short letter to Miss Burdett-Coutts, Dickens' philanthropic friend, a member of an immensely rich banking family. Dated 1 March, 1857, it went:

My dear Miss Coutts,

I do not see anything to object to in the accompanying report. You have done great good; an obviously bad thing is set right; although it would have been much better ingenuously done in the beginning than disingenuously, done it is, and many poor people will be the happier for it.

I will not fail to return the pamphlet on Common Things, and the corrections, in the course of the week.

Ever faithfully & aff. [affectionately] yours,

Charles Dickens

The scholarly footnote tells us (and the notes to this edition are models of their kind) that the report referred to in the letter is probably about a dead woman in St George's Hospital. No doubt the hospital, in the immemorial (and continuing) tradition of all institutions, had tried to cover up its failures and failings; Dickens and Miss Burdett-Coutts had succeeded in forcing a confession and a promise of reform.

A discovery just over a year ago by the great scholar of nineteenth century dissection, Ruth Richardson (her subject being a great deal more revealing of social history than might at first appear), has added greatly to the information contained in the short footnote to this letter – a proof, if one was needed, that no edition of anything as extensive as Dickens' correspondence is ever definitive.

Dr Richardson found that the case was that of Margaret Purvis, a poor widow who died of cancer in St George's Hospital (now a luxury hotel) aged 46. Her friend, Harriet Bragg, went to the hospital to collect the body, but was not allowed to enter what was called the dead-house, entry being reserved to the stronger sex. When the undertakers collected the body, however, they found it in a neglected state. It had never been properly laid out, and was stark naked on a slab with two naked men. Harriet Bragg, informed of this, enlisted Miss Burdett-Coutts who in turn enlisted Charles Dickens, who wrote to the governors of the hospital, eventually extracting from them the promise of reform.

Rationalists might say, I suppose, that what happens to a body after death little matters, and that therefore Miss Burdett-Coutts and Dickens were wasting their time. After all, it is what happens during life and before death that counts. There were surely worse abuses perpetrated against the living upon which these two philanthropists might have expended their time, albeit that Dickens was a man of volcanic energy: for even volcanoes are limited in their power of eruption.

But of course Dickens would have understood that the disrespect shown the body of Margaret Purvis was symbolic of and probably the continuation of the disrespect shown her before she died. To demand that respect be shown the bodies of the poor was to demand that respect was shown the poor while they lived: it was a kind of reverse engineering of general attitudes.

To demonstrate how far things had changed, the present deputy manager of the hospital's mortuary (which has moved to a less fashionable area of London) said in an interview that the dead are now treated as if they were still patients, not altogether as reassuring as intended in view of the presumed failure of the treatment they received in the hospital. He went on to say that the dead patients ('deceased' in his slightly euphemistic term, presumed to be gentler and more sensitive towards the mourning) were 'handled' with dignity and respect, the term 'handled' undoing all the attempted sensitivity of the word 'deceased.' And he continued 'It's a lot more clinical and everything's clean and tidy and all the bodies are refrigerated…' I am sure this was meant to be consolatory to all those whose relatives or loved ones had died in St George's Hospital, but somehow it rather misses the mark. The unfortunate deputy manager of the mortuary evidently has no way with words, which might suggest to the uncharitable that he has no way with feelings either: though this would perhaps be unfair. One probably ought not to expect eloquence from deputy managers of hospital mortuaries, though come to think of it why should it have been the deputy manager rather than the manager himself who was interviewed? Did the manager have something more pressing to do, or did he consider himself too grand a figure to sully himself by answering press enquiries? It is strange what disrespect one can read into little things.

Nearly a century and a half later there was a scandal in England over the body parts of babies who died in hospital and that were extracted for research and other purposes without the parents' permission. This had been the practice for decades. In English law, at least, a body is not anyone's property. But the possibility, virtually unknown in Dickens' and Miss Burdett-Coutts' day, of monetary compensation for distress suffered heightened the distress of those whose babies had been dissected in this way—for the law creates a vested interest in distress, the rule being the more distress, the more compensation.

Quite apart from the strange recurrence a hundred and fifty years later of a scandal over the disposal of the human body or its parts, Dickens' short letter illustrates how certain human propensities persist in very different circumstances and social conditions. He and Miss Burdett-Coutts evidently vanquished the resistance of the governors of St George's Hospital, whose first instinct was to defend the indefensible, which is and always will be the first instinct of practically all organisation men. This is not wholly unreasonable on their part because many critics are actuated only by temporary and evanescent moral enthusiasm and give up when their enthusiasm wanes. Defenders of the indefensible often have more at stake than attackers of the indefensible, and it is only when the attackers are as redoubtable as Dickens and Miss Burdett-Coutts that ground should be given.

Thus in history there is both change and constancy. No one would claim that nothing important had changed since Dickens' time, and changed in small part because of Dickens' own efforts. The treatment of the bodies of the poor, for example, did change after he and Miss Burdett-Coutts made their *démarche*. How far social change occurs because of deliberate political action and how far as the natural but unintended consequence of scientific and technological discovery, I am not sure: I suspect that the latter is much underestimated, especially by people of little scientific education or culture. But there is a level also at which nothing changes, or changes much, which is why we recognise the meaning of Dickens' letter when he says that it would have been better if the change had occurred ingenuously, that is to say without rear-guard action and from the simple recognition that it was necessary and right. Mankind is not so constituted, however; organisations no more than individuals change on the first conclusive intellectual proof or demonstration that they are mistaken, no more now than in Dickens' day. And this should help us be slightly less frustrated at or irritated with the intractable foolishness of our compeers, whom we no doubt frustrate or irritate in our turn.

While my hosts were out of the room I looked at the shelves of their library, extraordinarily rich in literary biography. I picked out a memoir of W. E. Henley, an all-but forgotten—but unjustly forgotten—poet about whom I wrote recently in an essay on poets with wooden legs. (Henley had one.) This was in part a satire on the tendency of modern literary scholars to classify and select authors by some politico-demographic criterion or other: sexual orientation, skin colour, etc.

Opening the book at page 4, the first words I read were as follows:

> Moreover Gloucester is so old a city and is so little changed that one can look to-day upon most of the very buildings that, for young Henley, gave life its setting.

This was written in 1930, but it couldn't possibly be written now. I almost cried as I read it. Gloucester has since been comprehensively destroyed, so that Henley would not have the faintest idea where he was, and is now only a glorious cathedral surrounded by a modernist slum. (Let no pedant point out that one or two mediaeval buildings remain: they serve only to emphasise the dispiriting slumminess of all that was built in the second half of the twentieth century, and in a way the survivals make everything worse by the starkness of the contrast.)

The destruction of old Gloucester was not the consequence of German bombing during the Second World War: Gloucester was little bombed. Indeed, the German bombing of Britain was much used by modernist architects and town planners as an excuse for doing what they wanted to do in any case: spit upon their ancestors for being so much better and more talented than they. It was the revenge of mediocrity upon talent and taste, and it continues to this day. After the war, much could have been rebuilt: but neither the people nor their governors cared enough for their aesthetic heritage to do so.

It is true that Gloucester had some appallingly crowded slums and some physically very squalid areas worthy of demolition: but the architects and planners made no distinction between a squalid slum tenement (which in the event they replaced by something just as bad, if bad in a different way) and a mediaeval priory or Georgian pump room. It was the latter, not the former, that they aimed at. It wasn't that they wanted to raise people up: they wanted to level them down. They wanted to create the New Man, that is to say the type who could not judge aesthetically of his own surroundings and therefore could aspire aesthetically to nothing. In large part they succeeded: I doubt that one person in a hundred in Gloucester notices just how terrible his city is. At best he will notice that the shops are not as good as in Cheltenham a few miles away.

The source of the modern hatred not of the injustice but of the achievements of the past is to me a subject of the greatest importance. It is a window on our souls.

I had only a few minutes in my hosts' library, itself but an infinitesimal part of any decent municipal library, let alone of that of Congress or the British Museum. In those few minutes I read only three or four sentences. There was obviously enough in that one room to stimulate a person for a lifetime, especially with the help of the internet. Now more than ever is what Pascal said true, that all of Mankind's problems derive from our inability to remain alone quietly in a room.

23
And Some Have Greatness Thrust From Them

THE PAST is another country where they do things differently: but how long past does the past have to be for the country to be utterly foreign? Sometimes it seems that the time that it takes is shorter and shorter, that a few years is more than sufficient. Who would have thought twenty years ago that the United States Supreme Court would be deliberating twenty years later as to whether it was actually legally permissible for any state of the union not to permit homosexual marriage? And this is so whether you now think that the whole idea is a good one or not.

I first realised how complete some changes in moral and social attitudes had been in my lifetime when I saw an old British black-and-white film, a comedy, about fifty years after it was made, in a cinema in a provincial town. In truth the film was not very good, and there was only one reason why I should remember it. There was a scene in which an upper class young man who had made a working-class girl pregnant was accosted by the girl's father and told that he would now have to marry her. The young man, much abashed, meekly agreed, and the audience howled with laughter—though this was, perhaps, the one scene in the film that was not supposed to be funny.

What a primitive notion that the father of a child had some inescapable duty towards not only it, but to its mother! It was as preposterous and alien to the audience as penny-farthing bicycles, as hilarious as the portrayal of typing pools. And I must admit that when I see typing pools, or even just someone sitting at a typewriter in an old film, a smile comes over me. How absurd to be stuck in the past, not to have moved with the times!

The audience evidently could not imagine a social world in which an unwanted pregnancy or a child born out of wedlock was some kind of catastrophe, and yet I, who am not quite ancient, remember it well. Why, even divorce was spoken of in those days in hushed tones, as if were a hateful infectious disease (which, of course, some people might say that it proved to be, so much so that it all but emptied marriage of meaning, except for the serious matter of divorce settlements).

Does the very swiftness of change mean that the literature even of the recent past will become in short order incomprehensible to new readers? When in Ireland, for example, I try to see plays, if any is playing, by a great modern playwright, John B Keane, who, rather unusually, was also for many years the landlord of a pub in Listowel. But his plays are about an Ireland that has disappeared almost entirely, an Ireland that I remember from my first visits there, impoverished and still largely rural, where the priest in a village or a town was morally if not economically a potentate whose word was law, and where the capital, Dublin, was a smoky, decaying place where warmth was to be found mainly in the pubs. It had a much stronger, more individual savour than it has now, but there was no denying that a grinding suffering caused by a cold poverty lay not far beneath the surface. Keane's plays depict an Ireland in which young girls could be more or less forcibly married by their parents to rich old men, wealth consisting of not much more than a few fields with pigs and cows, and perhaps a tractor. Good riddance to such a world, you might say, however propitious to the production of powerful literary artefacts such as Keane's plays (as often as not censored for a time). Ireland in a matter of a few decades has become a 'normal' modern country, and while much has been lost, more has been gained.

Keane's plays have suffered the terrible fate that awaits so much of recent literature that depicts a recently-vanished world: they have become part of the school syllabus. But how much can they really mean to children who have grown up without fear of local marriage brokers, for whom sex has lost, not its interest of course, but its fears and terrors, its associated guilt and furtiveness, and for whom the struggle over a small piece of infertile land as if it were a matter of life and death was as alien as, say, the sacrificial practices of the Aztecs, and for whom the priest has no particular authority, rather the reverse of authority? At an excellent performance of Keane's most famous play, Sive, which is searing in its intensity, I watched a group of schoolchildren who had come because the play was a set work for this year's public examination. They were healthy, lively children, full of gaiety (as, of course, they should have been): but what could the travelling tinker in the play, who supplies a kind of Cassandra-like chorus to the action, have signified to them? When Keane wrote the play in the 1950s there were still tinkers who travelled the byways of the country, half-entertaining and half-scaring the settled population into providing for them, their curses on those who gave them nothing being no laughing matter to those on whom they were placed. The nearest to this any of the children might have come was cyber-bullying on Facebook.

On the other hand, it is precisely the ability of literature to enable us imaginatively to enter the lives of others that is its glory, or at any rate one of its glories, an ability that does not depend on whether or not we have ever experienced the outward conditions or circumstances of the characters. We need to know very little history to be moved by Richard II's speeches, for example, and though we have never been kings ourselves, or been deposed from a throne, yet the speeches he makes as Bolingbroke overthrows him have a universal significance, or at least a significance for anyone who has known a fall. Indeed there is a profound egalitarian message in Richard II: not the type of equality struggled for by demagogic politicians, but the one that underlies all human existence. We are born, we live, we die, and that while we live we are troubled by the same concerns as everyone else. King Richard moves us (all the more so, as Shakespeare has not loaded the dice in his favour by making him a good or admirable man) when he says:

> Cover your heads and mock not flesh and blood
> With solemn reverence: throw away respect,
> Tradition, form and ceremonious duty,
> For you have but mistook me all this while:
> I live with bread like you, feel want,
> Taste grief, need friends: subjected thus,
> How can you say to me, I am a king?

Surely this is a call to modesty to all those who imagine themselves placed either by circumstance or by their own efforts above others? That, no matter how high we rise, we are all Richard II? That, in effect, no man can be a king, if by king we mean someone who is absolved of all human cares?

On a shelf in a dusty antique centre, where kitsch is mixed promiscuously with elegant eighteenth century furniture, I found a small volume by an author, Stanley Houghton, of whom I had not previously heard. What induced me to pick it up I cannot say, except that these days I am much in favour of short books. It was a play titled *Hindle Wakes*, and as soon as I started to read I was as if captured. I wanted to hurry home and finish it, as well as find out about the author in that great library, the internet.

The play takes place in Edwardian Lancashire. The son of the rich local cotton mill owner, an amiable but shallow semi-ne'er-do-well, has gone on a weekend to the seaside with the daughter of a mill worker. According to the standards of the time, he has 'ruined' her and is morally obliged to marry her, though at the time of his seaside jaunt he was engaged to be married to the daughter of another rich mill owner. The young man's father has risen from the bottom, having gone to work in a factory at the age of eight, before rising to his present wealth and eminence; and the the mill worker whose daughter his son has 'ruined,' who has remained a simple worker in his own mill, was a childhood friend of his.

The characters are extremely well-delineated. The mill-owner is a man of superior intelligence with a forceful and determined, not to say domineering, personality, so that his social ascent is fully plausible; but he also has a kind of unbending moral probity that impels him to do what is right even if it is against his own interests to do so, the kind of probity that was a part of the culture of non-conformist (that is to say, non-Anglican) protestant religion—a culture that, to all intents and purposes, is now extinct. The subtlety of Houghton's delineation lies in the combination of the mill-owner's probity and his determination never to be thwarted once he has set his mind on something, in this case the marriage of his son to the woman whom he has dishonoured. Inflexible probity becomes a form of spiritual pride; by contrast, the father of the dishonoured girl, by no means unintelligent, is flexible (or is it weak?) and understanding. His wife, the mother of the girl, after initially having been appalled by her 'dishonour,' sees in it a splendid chance for her to marry into money.

Throughout the twists and turns of the plot, or rather of the relations between the characters and their psychological plausibility, one remains eager to know the denouement, and even after it has taken place there is just enough ambiguity to keep you wondering. It is a most impressive play, entertaining, not in the least didactic, but not trivial either.

But of course its emotional impact depends entirely upon the playgoers' ability to understand and even empathise with the assumption that for an unmarried girl to spend a weekend with a man is a terrible scandal that will permanently damage or ruin her reputation. Without this premise, all the agonising will seem pointless, rather as arcane theological disputes of the fourth century AD seem to unbelievers. Suffice it to say that the prevailing sexual mores of 1912, when *Hindle Wakes* was written and first performed, were not those of a century later, to put it mildly; and though, allegedly, we live in a multicultural age, which in practice means that we like lots of different kinds of food, I am not sure that an age of Facebook and Twitter is one that is propitious to the grasping of outlooks other than one's own. So absorbed are we in the vast continent of the present moment that we are increasingly unable to travel imaginatively to the foreign land of the past.

I might be wrong, and hope that I am. I would like to give *Hindle Wakes* to adolescents to read to discover whether they would be puzzled by it, find it ridiculous, or understand the drama contained in it.

No such experiment would be conclusive, of course. If the young people did not find the play compelling in any way, this might be attributed to the dramatist's failure to communicate well enough. There is, presumably, a reason why Stanley Houghton is not a household name, even among ardent theatre-goers.

He was an interesting and tragic figure, though. Born in 1881, he worked in his father's business as a cloth merchant in Manchester practically all his short adult life. But he was a keen amateur actor and was much influenced in his writing by Ibsen, as of course was Bernard Shaw (but Houghton's characters speak like men, unlike Shaw's, who speak like abstractions made vaguely humanoid). He wrote several plays that are apparently of considerable quality, and with the commercial success of *Hindle Wakes* threw up his job in his father's firm and went to live in Paris, where he wrote six chapters of a novel before falling fatally ill of pneumonia and meningitis and dying at the age of 32. Of course, had he survived, he might have been killed in the First World War instead; but had he survived it, he would have written a truly great work. Chance plays it part even in the achievement of greatness.

24
Graves' Disease?

ROBERT GRAVES (1895 – 1985) was one of the few men who was able to read his own obituary, albeit sixty-nine years before he actually died. He was badly injured in the First World War and left for dead; the Times published an obituary on this mistaken belief.

His most famous books are his memoir of that war, *Good-bye to All That*, published in 1929, a title that captures in four words the profound change wrought by that cataclysm; and *I, Claudius*, an historical novel, published in 1934, that was turned into a very successful television drama serial. But he was a man of many parts, who wrote among other things a slim volume with the title *Lars Porsena: On the Future of Swearing*. I doubt he realised just how prosperous the future of swearing would be, in quantity if not necessarily in quality.

His personal life was colourful, to say the least; he lived for many years and died on the island of Majorca, and was the subject of this amusing clerihew:

> When Robert Graves
> Misbehaves,
> It's the talka
> Majorca.

For some people, at least, he was an inexhaustible subject of conversation.

Graves thought of himself as primarily a poet. One of his last volumes, *Poems 1968 – 1970*, seems full of foreboding about his impending descent into dementia, which he suffered for at least the last ten years of his life. In *The Imminent Seventies* he writes:

> Are not all centuries, like men,
> Born hopeful too and gay,
> And good for seventy years, but then
> Hope slowly seeps away?

This was written, of course, before the English language was deprived of the word *gay* in any but its present sense, all other senses being as finally extinguished as the first name Adolf throughout Europe and the world.

Graves gives us a version of Shakespeare's seventh age of man, that:

> … second childishness and mere oblivion,
> Sans teeth, sans eyes, sans taste, sans everything.

Graves' version goes:

> True, a new geriatric art
> Prolongs our last adventures
> When eyes grow dim, when teeth depart:
> For glasses come, and dentures –

And indeed Graves, who had written 140 books, wrote no more in the last ten years of his life.

The only consolation for Graves was that fame in old age no longer invited envy or backbiting. He ends *Troublesome Fame*, about the pitfalls and difficulties that much sought-after but oft-regretted commodity, by the following stanza:

> But Fame attendant on extreme old age
> Falls best. What envious youth cares to compete
> With a lean sage hauled painfully upstage,
> Bowing, gasping, shuffling his frozen feet –
> A ribboned hearse parked plainly down the street?

There is one poem in the collection that particularly caught my attention, and that intersected with my clinical interests, called *Man of Evil*. This is a poem—not, I think great poetry—about that hero of an ever-growing number of films, the psychopath. How are we to conceive of evil, a word that many philosophers have declared redundant, as doctors have declared redundant the word hysteria, but which returns like the proverbial bad penny, and that we are strangely unable to do without?

Graves starts with a question:

> But should I not pity that poor devil,
> Such a load of guilt he carries?

This might seem at first sight contradictory, for it is one of the principal characteristics of the psychopath that he feels no guilt. That, after all, was why the British physician, John Cowles Prichard, coined the term 'moral insanity' for it. The sufferer from this condition, or at least the person who made others suffer from it, seemed to be perfectly normal in his mentation except for an absence of moral sense—an absence which, of course, affected his emotional responses to events.

But in my experience, at least, such people are aware of the moral judgments of others and can enumerate moral principles as well as the next man; they are just unable to feel them from the inside, as it were, they cannot experience them. They are like a critic who mouths enthusiasm for something without feeling it, because he knows that the weight of critical opinion is in its favour. To break ranks is dangerous.

In that sense, then, the psychopath may bear a weight of guilt: he has to explain away his evil deeds to an audience who, for some reason unknown to him, seems to demand an explanation. Graves gets this right: having enumerated the protagonist's deeds—debauching the daughter of his benefactor, drug-dealing, a first wife driven mad, a second drowned in a pond in mysterious and unelucidated circumstances—the psychopath then explains, or explains away:

> He complains always of his luckless childhood
> And fills commiserating eyes with tears…
>
> He cowers and sponges when his guilt is plain
> And his bank-account runs dry.
> O, that unalterable black self-pity,
> Void of repentance or amendment,
> Clouding his Universe!

But in the midst of this, Graves tells us that:

> The truth is: he was evil from the womb
> And both his parents knew it.

And certainly I have met people who, as soon as they were able to exercise conscious choice, opted always for the worst. They were cruel to animals, put cats in the washing machine and acid in the goldfish bowl, lied for no reason except for the pleasure of deceit, and in general pursued a mirror-image of Kant's categorical imperative. In so far as at least some of these individuals were brought up in a normal way, not different from their siblings who were in no way psychopathic, their propensity to evil seemed to be, if not genetic, at least congenital. And if it were, could they be called evil? Graves' title, *Man of Evil*, suggests that the deeds rather than the person who commits them is where the evil lies: although he had long given up his Christian faith (lost in the First World War), enough remained for him to distinguish in his heart between the sin and the sinner.

For a man himself to be evil, he has to choose to do evil in spite of knowing it to be wrong and be capable of not doing it. *Ex hypothesi*, the man outlined above is not evil—he is, as Dr Prichard would have called him, morally insane. For him, evil is as the flame to the moth: and who blames moths? Such men are not many (there are even fewer women of this ilk), but they exist.

Are there any that do evil, or even wrong, knowingly? Socrates thought not, that wrongdoing was the result of ignorance. If we but knew the right, we should do it. This is against the experience of the vast majority of mankind, most of which will have done wrong knowingly and which will have known others to have done wrong knowingly.

The humble activity of clearing up the roadside also proves that Socrates was mistaken: it is not ignorance that leads people to do wrong, but the placing of minor convenience or pleasure above all other considerations that does so.

My wife and I, tired of waiting for the council to do its duty and clean the lanes around our beautiful little town of litter, have taken to cleaning them ourselves. It is futile in a way, for the task is far too great for us alone: we can clear about 200 yards on both sides of the road in 45 minutes, thereby gathering two substantial sacks of litter. It is not unsatisfying work though, for it is far from unpleasant if the weather is clement and the result is immediately visible.

The point is, however, that many people have gone to the trouble to insinuate their litter deep into the hedge-row, from which it is difficult to retrieve it; moreover, they almost certainly have waited until there was no one around to see them do it. In other words, they knew perfectly well that what they were doing was wrong, but chose to do it anyway.

The people who behave in this way, I suspect, are not at all the type of people I have described above. They are far too numerous for that, and if all the people who did it were true psychopaths the murder rate would be a hundred or a thousand times higher than it is. Having more of a choice, then, than those who suffer from congenital moral insanity, are they in fact worse people than the latter? Their crimes are less serious but more numerous. How many small crimes make a large one? If there is no common unit of badness, so that, for example, one murder without extenuation would equal a thousand Hitler units, while dropping a chocolate wrapper would equal one Hitler unit, such that a thousand dropped wrappers would equal one murder, how could one ever compare, at least scientifically, the badness of acts? If the answer is moral intuition, the door to relativism is opened: for my moral intuition is not the same as yours and may even be diametrically opposed to it. Whose intuition is to prevail? And yet, when we say that a certain action is bad, we are not merely saying I don't approve of it: we believe, on the contrary, that we are making a judgment that corresponds to a reality independent of our mental state.

All these problems are too difficult for me, I gave up on them a long time ago, only for Graves' poem to come along and resuscitate them in my mind.

His last stanza seems to me interesting, if slightly confused. It goes:

> But who can cast out evil? We can only
> Learn to diagnose that natal sickness,
> The one known cure for which, so far, is death.
> Evil is here to stay unendingly,
> But so also is Love.

When Graves asks who can cast out evil, he seems to be referring to the whole of Mankind, in effect to Original Sin. Clearly it is unrealistic to expect a human existence without evil, for even if we are not born to it, exactly, we are certainly born to the capacity for it. As to those—few in number—who seem to be born to nothing else, death is not always the only cure: they seem sometimes to mature out of their moral insanity.

But the last two lines are the most curious: for in them Graves opposes not good to evil, but love. And in doing so, he is very modern indeed, despite his age at the time and the fact that he grew up an Edwardian.

A lack of love may certainly be a psychological source of evil where it is not congenital; but that does not mean that love is itself the antonym of evil, either in common parlance or in philosophy. It might be difficult to imagine a person who could not love to be capable of doing right, but that does not mean that love is coterminous with the good. Indeed, it is perfectly possible to imagine people doing evil for the sake of love. Indeed, *An Evil Love* is the title of a book written about Fred and Rose West, two notorious serial killers, who kidnapped young women to torture them sexually and then kill them.

The opposition of love to evil in effect empties the notion of good of almost all its rational quality, for it is notorious that love is like the wind, it bloweth where it listeth. If love justifies actions and makes them necessarily good, then to be good is merely an emotional state. And this is very gratifying because it requires no discipline at all, no suppression of inclinations, so long as they can be said to arise from love.

In another poem, *In the Name of Virtue*, Graves says:

> Virtue is from listening
> To a private angel,
> An angel overheard
> When the little-finger twitches –
> The bold little-finger
> That refused education:
> When the rest went to college
> And philosophized on Virtue,
> It neither went nor tried.

How easy life becomes when virtue consists of listening to your inner angel!

> Knowing becomes doing
> When all you need to know
> Is how to check our pendulum
> And move the hands around
> For a needed golden instant…

Are poets the unacknowledged legislators of the world?

25
Doing the Charleston

'IN STATELY OLD Charleston,' ran a headline in a recent edition of the *New York Times*, 'New Buildings on the Block Are Struggling to Fit In.' This is a very strange way of putting it: for it reverses the relation between Man and his own productions.

Buildings cannot struggle, not even metaphorically: they are not like fish in the talons of an eagle or a wart hog attacked by a lion. Admittedly one does not look to the *Times* for elegance of writing, perhaps not even for mere accuracy, though its layout looks as if it was designed by a professor of Aramaic philology at the University of Gottingen in about 1880. Pedantic layout, loose (though dull) writing: that more or less summarizes the *Times*.

What the headlines meant, I think, is that architects and city planners were trying—or struggling, to use the Times' more sensationalist word—to find a style of modern architecture that harmonised aesthetically with Charleston's eighteenth and nineteenth century buildings. My guesses are a) that they won't find it, and b) that they won't try very hard.

Let me briefly return to the locution of 'buildings struggling,' that so deftly evades the fact that buildings do not design and erect themselves but require human beings to do both of those things (and not *for them*, either, for that would imply that buildings had intentions). I am reminded of Le Corbusier's exclamation, 'The plan, the plan must rule!' First, of course, he provided no coherent explanation as to *why* the plan must rule: his writings are long strings of *ex cathedra* statements connected by no logic whatsoever and whose main interest is why anyone should have taken them seriously. To answer that question would require an examination of the zeitgeist in which they were received, which for the moment I shall leave aside.

'The plan must rule!' This way of putting it also disguises that plans do not make themselves, nor can they rule. What Le Corbusier meant was 'I must plan and I must rule.' His plan, incidentally, was for architecture in the whole world: not bad for a boy from a little town in Switzerland (or anywhere else, for that matter).

No doubt there are many instances in which the desires of men are transformed by language into impersonal imperatives, over which human purpose reigns no more than it does over a tsunami produced by an earthquake at the bottom of the ocean. It is one of the tasks of the citizen, certainly of the intellectual, to unmask this disguise, whether that disguise be conscious or unconscious.

Now to return to the question of how hard the architects and city planners will 'struggle' to make new buildings fit in. This has not exactly been the obsession of architects in the recent past. On the contrary, their struggle has been more to make sure that their productions have been noticed or could not go unnoticed. No one, for example, who looked at the Pompidou Centre in Paris would think that the architects had made any effort to blend their building with whatever was all around it, or with Paris in general, rather the reverse. They wanted it to strike the eye like a punch in the face, and in this they certainly succeeded. Success in pursuit of a bad goal, however, is much more to be lamented than failure.

The question naturally arises as to why anyone would choose the goal that the architects of the Pompidou Centre chose: to which, I think, the answer is the egotism of architects, itself only a manifestation of a general social (or antisocial) inclination to egotism. In an age of celebrity, in which people feel anonymity as a wound, as an insult to their ego, they feel the need to do whatever is necessary to stand out in some way, whether it be by dress or conduct, or—in the case of architects—by building something that stands out, albeit like an red ink-stain on an etching by Rembrandt. We are all artists now, even if we have no talent (except for self-promotion, the most important of all talents): and, as everyone knows, no one is an artist who is not original. The more a building clashes with its surroundings, then, the more original, and artistic, is the architect. The humility necessary genuinely to seek harmony with what already exists is not the first characteristic of architects of today. The jobbers among them care for nothing but their fees, the more ambitious for fame or notoriety. Better to be hated than unnoticed: indeed, given that some great artist (though actually rather few) went derided in their lifetime, excoriation is for some a validation of their work. I'm hated, therefore I'm good.

As it happens, I had a discussion in my local pub recently with a young man—I now think of 40 year-olds as young men—about architecture. He had grown to adult consciousness at a time when virtually all urban architectural harmony in his native country, Britain, had been wilfully destroyed by modernists who could, for reasons I have not the space to go into, leave nothing untouched, but whose logic was that of Macbeth. To adapt very slightly that character's words, every British modernist could have said:

> I am in ugliness
> Stepp'd in so far that, were I to wade no more,
> Returning were as tedious as to go o'er.

To stop their work of destruction would be an admission of guilt, and that they will never make.

My young interlocutor saw no virtue in harmony: rather he saw it in contrast. Of course, since harmony is not the same as uniformity, contrast can be, and often is, both interesting and graceful. But he was for contrast as clash rather than harmony: a gastronomic equivalent would perhaps be smoked eel and chocolate mousse on the same plate, or more to the point foie gras and a Krispy Kreme Donut (the latter appalling under any circumstances whatever).

Perhaps the difference between us was most evident when I mentioned that the city council of Bath, the once-fashionable Eighteenth Century spa town, intended in the 1950s to pull practically all the old buildings and replace them with the modern architecture of that aesthetically dispiriting epoch (modernity is, of course, the most fleeting of qualities). Fortunately the townspeople, or a large number of them, had better instincts than their elected representatives, and civic action halted the council's barbaric plans—but not before 4000 Georgian houses, workmen's cottages for the most part that would now probably sell for $800,000 each, had been pulled down to make way for ugly utilitarian constructions.

My interlocutor said something that should not have surprised me, but nevertheless shocked me. He said he did not in the least mind the loss of 4000 Georgian houses because there were so many still standing anyway, all round the country. On this kind of logic, it would not matter if one pulled down mediaeval palaces in Venice, so long as some of them remained: nor would it matter what one put in their place, so long presumably as whatever it was sufficiently contrasting.

On one thing we were able to agree: that modern pastiche of eighteenth century architecture was often terrible, at least in Britain: but this, I said, was because, for one reason or another, pride perhaps, architects were unwilling to use the model correctly. As an instance, I gave the proportions of the windows: almost invariably, pastiche gets it wrong, though nothing could be easier than to get it right.

Now here my interlocutor said something was at least partly true and revealing: he said that the architects did not follow the proportions of the windows because of considerations of energy efficiency. And this I could well believe: in a climate like ours, it takes more energy to heat a room with large and generously-proportioned windows than with mean and narrow ones.

But note that here the premise of the argument against building in the Georgian style of architecture has changed. It is not that we do not want to build like the Georgians for aesthetic, but rather for narrowly utilitarian, reasons. We want to be kept warm as cheaply as possible. Whereas we were once asked to celebrate the new aesthetic as being in some way superior to the old on aesthetic grounds alone, we are now told that we cannot adhere to the old aesthetic for reasons of conservation of energy. If it were not for those considerations, then, we should be only too delighted to build as they built.

As would be perfectly possible for us, though almost certainly expensive. On the other hand, are we not supposed to be the richest people who ever lived? How comes it, then, that the Georgians were able to build 4000 elegant (though no doubt cramped) cottages for workers, that probably housed at least 12,000 people, that is to say the equivalent of 84,000 people today, in one city alone, while we are incapable with all our wealth and technical brio of building anything remotely as fine, but are capable only of demolition? An architectural historian once said to me that it was simply because our building methods and materials had changed, but this answer left me dissatisfied on two counts: first that modernism is generally celebrated on account of its aesthetic, not on the grounds that it is the only style consonant with our new building methods and materials, and second that I find it impossible to believe that, with sufficient will to do so, we could not have found a way of mass-producing elegance by means other than the Georgians used. Our problem is not our methods but our priorities and our taste.

One of the things that most struck me about my interlocutor was what one might call his aesthetic pointillism. Each tiny portion of a townscape was for him individual and unrelated to any other. Thus for him it would not be a sacrilege to erect a Dubai-style skyscraper in the middle of Venice on the grounds that it would destroy the aesthetic unity of the city (which, of course, is very far from that of a unity of style of individual buildings). The loss would not be irreparable because the vast majority of the city would remain intact. Needless to say, no heritage could long survive this pointillism: it is aesthetic barbarism.

Another aspect of his aesthetics was historicism. When I said that British architecture of recent decades has been uniformly dreadful (of course an exaggeration, but a very slight one) he asked me about the Lloyds Building in the City of London. I said that it was an elaborate mess, an eyesore, whose originality was one of its great and many defects. He admitted that it was not nice to look at but, he added, I (that is to say I the author of this article) was forced to admit that it was ahead of its time. I said this was a worthless criterion by which to judge architecture: it was like saying that Houston Stewart Chamberlain or Edouard Drumont were good writers because they were ahead of their time, that is to say as nineteenth century intellectual progenitors of Nazism. His remark also reminded me of what Rossini once said of Wagner, that his music was better than it sounded. Architecture, being a relatively permanent and certainly very obtrusive art form (if it is an art form at all), it must be judged by what it is here and now, not what it foreshadows. To a small extent you may judge a book or a picture by that criterion, because no one has to hang the picture on his wall or read the book: but a building is not like that. It forces itself on you, unless you blindfold yourself either literally or metaphorically.

Our conversation depressed me, though I soon wondered why it should. After all, I will be leaving this world sooner than he; and if he and his descendants do not mind the destruction of the heritage of the past, why should I who will soon no longer be present to enjoy it?

But still I grieve for what is likely to happen—or rather be done—to Charleston.

26
Falstaff the Brave

I LOVE TO READ about Shakespeare, in part because to do so is so perfectly pointless. A man cannot always be engaged in useful activity, for something has to be pursued for its own sake and without ulterior motive; and reading about Shakespeare is both harmless and inexhaustible. It would take an entire lifetime to read the works of the Baconians alone, of those who believe that Shakespeare the poet and playwright was not Shakespeare the boy from Stratford-upon-Avon, but rather Francis Bacon, Lord Verulam.

What they write is often—no, almost always—formidably erudite, though a slight air of madness usually hangs over it. The founder of the school, the American Delia Bacon (1811 - 1859), did end her days in an asylum, but that, I admit, is no argument against Baconianism.

One cannot help but feel admiration and even affection for such people, who work so hard to prove something of no economic value to themselves and purely for the love of knowledge, if perhaps tinged by a desire to score against those whom they call with an unmistakable condescension the Stratfordians, the naïve believers in the identity of Shakespeare the poet and playwright and Shakespeare the boy from Stratford-upon-Avon.

Over the years, without really meaning to, I have accumulated quite a little Baconian library, buying their books whenever I happen across them. They are written by many different types: an Irish Jesuit, an English judge, a large landowner, an aged surgeon and anatomist who was said to have committed all the works of both Bacon and Shakespeare, which of course he believed to be by the same person, to memory so that he could collate them, publishing his book in the middle of the

Second World War not long before he died; but perhaps my favourite among them for sheer magnificence of folly is Dr Orville Ward Owen, a doctor from Detroit, who in the 1890s persuaded himself by means of a cipher machine that Bacon was Shakespeare and moreover that, also revealed by cipher in the works of the Bard, his manuscripts lay hidden at the bottom of the River Wye at Chepstow, which he proceeded to dredge at great and ruinous expense to himself, of course finding nothing. He also wrote history plays in what he persuaded himself was the style of Shakespeare. Alas poor man, he died both disillusioned and impoverished, wishing that he had never taken up the subject of the authorship of Shakespeare. Indeed, he was a character of Shakespearean dimension; his life is worthy of study for its failure and for its lesson that we often arrive at predetermined conclusions by methods which we delude ourselves are objective.

The theory that Bacon was Shakespeare (or is it that Shakespeare was Bacon?) unleashed the dogs of detection, and before long there were other candidates for the honour of having been the greatest author in the history of the world, among them Christopher Marlow, the Earl of Rutland and, the current favourite I believe, the Earl of Oxford. They too have had their immensely learned proponents, most notably the founder of the Oxfordians, the unfortunately-named J. Thomas Looney. I have always thought that intellectual snobbery was part of the motive for the work of the anti-Stratfordians, who at least subliminally dislike the notion that the greatest author in the history of the world was not highly educated, or at least attended no university, which seems somehow against the natural order of things. Perhaps one day a society will be formed to prove that Bill Gates was not the real founder of Microsoft, on the grounds that he never completed a university degree in information technology.

There are whole libraries on every aspect of Shakespeare, from his biography to his bibliography, from his pathography to his punctuation, from his topography to his typography. There are books about his knowledge of botany, seamanship, navigation, soldiering, law and medicine, and many other things as well. There are fewer books about Shakespeare and medicine than about Shakespeare and the law, but nonetheless a very large number. Sir John Charles Bucknill, founder of the journal that was to become the *British Journal of Psychiatry*, started the genre with books such as *The Mad Folk of Shakespeare, The Psychology of Shakespeare* and *The Medical Knowledge of Shakespeare*. The last of these books is a powerful call to modesty, for Bucknill wrote it at a time when real medical knowledge, by our standards, was exiguous, but Bucknill nevertheless judged Shakespeare's knowledge by his own standards and some of his judgments now seem distinctly bizarre.

But all these books are as nothing compared with critical and interpretative studies: the municipal library of a small town in the Mid-West compared to the Library of Congress. Again without intending to have done so, I have accumulated (rather than collected) a small library on the meaning of the Sonnets, from Samuel Butler who found them entirely homosexual to A. L. Rowse, who claimed definitively to have identified the Dark Lady, and who spent much of the last part of his very long life pouring petulant and unpleasant scorn on those who did not agree with him.

Hazlitt warns us against the futility of Shakespearean criticism (to which, of course, he added himself). I know what he means: there are furious and often intemperate debates over the meaning of, say, *Hamlet*, that seem to forget altogether that *Hamlet* is actually a work of fiction. (A favourite work of mine is *Hamlet and the Philosophy of Literary Criticism* by Morris Weitz.) But such is the force of Shakespeare's human genius, as Hazlitt calls it, that his characters often seem more real to us, and occupy our imaginations more fully, than do many of our acquaintances. I have found that if one calls Mrs Clinton Lady Macbeth, very little remains to be said and everyone knows precisely what one means. Morbid jealousy has been called Othello Syndrome, we know exactly what to expect of someone called Falstaffian, and Romeo stands for young love the world over. The psychotherapist, Dr Murray Cox, who practised at Britain's main institution for the criminally insane, Broadmoor, used Shakespeare in his work and said that there was no aspect of his patients' states of mind that was unilluminated by Shakespeare—whose work he knew like the proverbial back of his hand.

But life being for pleasure rather than use, Dr Cox would still have been a great Shakespearean even had he found no utility in his knowledge. And I derive pleasure from books about Shakespeare even if they extend the scope of my knowledge only a little, or rather the scope of my amnesia: for I have reached the age when it is information in, twice as much out.

Recently I happened on a short book, famous among real scholars of Shakespeare criticism, titled *An Essay on the Dramatic Character of Sir John Falstaff* by Maurice Morgann, published in 1777. I had been writing an essay on Falstaff myself, but I did not read Morgann until I had finished, for sometimes other people's ideas muddle rather than clear one's own. I like when writing about a play or character in Shakespeare to take a line or two that I use, legitimately or not, as a key to the whole: for example, 'you would pluck out the heart of my mystery' for Hamlet and 'Nor are those empty-hearted whose low sounds/ Reverb no hollowness' for King Lear. And for Falstaff, I used 'Banish plump Jack, and banish all the world.'

Having finished my little essay, I read Morgann's much more substantial effort with unalloyed pleasure, though the main idea that he propounded did not entirely convince me: that Falstaff was not a coward, at least not a coward by nature. His apparent cowardice, according to Morgann, was more in the nature of prudence, though he does not go so far as to claim that it was prudence exercised in any but for personal survival.

When, for example, Falstaff lays down and plays dead in the course of his brief conflict with Douglas, thus saving his own life, Morgann says that he is merely being sensible, for what good would his certain death at Douglas' hands have served? He, Falstaff, was nearly seventy years old, his experience as a soldier had taught him that rashness in the name of honour was foolish; and indeed one of the first jingles I ever learned was 'He who fights and runs away/ Lives to fight another day.'

By a closer reading of the text than I had performed, Morgann demonstrates, or claims to demonstrate, that Falstaff was no coward, that what little we know of his previous life (for example from Justice Shallow) suggests the contrary, and that indeed his being given command of foot soldiers, almost all of whom are killed in battle, proves that Prince Hal could not really have thought of him as such. Morgann does not claim that Falstaff was without other vices, but as he justly remarks, boastful lies are boastful lies, not cowardice; he does not consider whether a propensity to boastful lying about fighting exploits is more common among cowards than among the brave. In any case, a statistical correlation between cowardice and boastfulness would not go to prove that Falstaff was a coward, for you cannot justly infer individual characteristics from group ones. From the fact that the Dutch are the tallest people in the world you cannot deduce that a man is not Dutch because he is not tall.

Morgann sets out to overturn the prejudices of all common readers of Falstaff who, like me, take Falstaff's cowardice for granted. Does he not, in addition to playing dead for Douglas, run away from Gads Hill after only token resistance to his assailants? Morgann has a good answer for that, too, in defence of Falstaff's natural courage. And yet one is not convinced.

Morgann tells us that he is not writing for those who are so prejudiced that they cannot or will not change their minds in the face of the evidence. This is a subtle rhetorical move, for it predisposes you to change your mind in order to prove that you are not one of the incurably prejudiced. Nevertheless, I at any rate began at once to think of objections to Morgann's thesis in order not to have to change my mind, which is always a painful thing to have to do. Nor should one give up one's prejudices lightly, at the first sign of evidence to their contrary. Prejudices are like spouses, they should not be divorced at the first approach of trouble: though eventually complete incompatibility may necessitate divorce. Throughout his essay, for example, Morgann takes the statements of Falstaff and others much too literally, and does not consider that statements might sometimes be meant ironically rather than literally.

Morgann was by all accounts an amiable man and historically an important one: he was the British signatory of the peace with America. He also predicted future trouble in America with slavery, which he detested, and against which he wrote a strong pamphlet. But his *Essay*, by far his best-known work (which called forth a sarcastic response from Dr Johnson who said that he now looked forward to an essay proving that Iago was a good man), was written, according to the author himself, purely for the intellectual pleasure of proving something of no importance. He wrote it for his own and other people's pleasure, and for no other reason.

Actually, I think that here he was not being quite frank. Just as even the most cynical of hack journalists harbours the faint hope that a few of his pages might survive his death, so Morgann had a sneaking hope that his little book had more significance than he earlier claims for it. He finishes it as follows:

> So… ends an Essay, on which the reader is left to bestow what character he pleases: an Essay, professing to treat of the courage of Falstaff, but extending itself to his whole character; to the arts and genius of his poetic maker, SHAKESPEARE; and through him sometimes, with ambitious aim, even to the principles of human nature.

I suspect that even the reporter of weddings for local newspapers secretly hopes as much.

27
All Men Are Created Snobs

IT IS A SAD FACT that many distinguished men, who in their time seemed to bestride the world like colossi and excited anything from extreme admiration to the utmost detestation, but who never evoked mere indifference (if indifference, that is, needs to be evoked at all, rather than being merely our default attitude to the majority of our fellow beings), are no sooner dead than forgotten. As Richard II puts it, rather more eloquently than can I:

> … within the hollow crown
> That rounds the mortal temples of a king
> Keeps Death his court and there the antic sits,
> Scoffing his state and grinning at his pomp,
> Allowing him a breath, a little scene,
> To monarchize, be fear'd and kill with looks,
> Infusing him with self and vain conceit,
> As if this flesh which walls about our life,
> Were brass impregnable, and humour'd thus
> Comes at the last and with a little pin
> Bores through his castle wall, and farewell king!

Collective amnesia, indeed, can set in even before a distinguished man's death, and that seems to have happened in the case of Robert Ranulph Marett, a festschrift for whom, published on the occasion of his 70th birthday in 1936, I bought recently. He was never exactly a household name, having been a social anthropologist in Oxford and the head of a college there, but he was the student and teacher of many men more famous than he (in so far as anthropologists *can* be famous) and the two pictures of him in the book, one of a portrait painting and the other an inserted loose photograph of him showing the Alake of Egbaland (the king of a kingdom in Western Nigeria) around Oxford, the Alake, a cheerful and splendid figure in magnificent robes, his wife behind him, the Queen, looking as glum as Mrs Obama in Saudi Arabia, indicate a highly distinguished man fully aware of his own distinction. He is confident of his position and importance in the world, and yet he was by then already in the process of being side-lined even from his own academic discipline. The *Dictionary of National Biography* says of the festschrift:

> ... the majority of the contributors... make no reference to his work, and those that do mention it do so merely as a brief, preliminary courtesy.

Immensely gifted, vastly erudite, he is now forgotten; as the Dictionary puts with a frankness painful to all authors who hope they will still be read after their deaths, but who are not half as gifted or erudite as was he, 'Few, however, read Marett's works today.' They are truly at one with Nineveh and Tyre.

I probably should not have bought the book, titled *Custom Is King: Essays Presented to R. R. Marett*, had it not been Marett's own copy, bearing his signature in the confident hand of a distinguished man. Even then, I dickered over buying it (it is strange how we waste thousands in our lives without a second thought and then ponder deeply over spending a small amount of loose change), for I find social anthropology, which ought to be so interesting, almost impossible to read. And indeed, many of the titles of the essays were of positively Saharan dryness, for example *The Modern Growth of the Totem-Pole on the North-West Coast*, or *An Interesting Naga-Melanesian Culture-link*. Even the mildly salacious title, *Kinship, Incest and Exogamy of the Northern Territories of the Gold Coast*, is misleading. I doubt that many readers could get past:

> The basis of filiation is the agnatic lineage. Four degrees of lineal filiation may be noted here, though many more degrees function in practice.

Of fundamentally frivolous nature, I would find *Sodomy in the Supreme Court* or *Wife-Beating in Buckingham Palace* more interesting.

Still there were one or two things of interest even in all this weary pedantry. Marett was not a humourless man, he was fond of anecdotes and once had a public discussion 'as to the credibility of [the story of] a missionary to the cannibal islands who "became ultimately absorbed in his work:"' that is to say eaten and absorbed in the digestive sense. It so happens that, more than forty years later, when I was just setting out for the South Seas, I met a man who claimed that a great-uncle of his, also a missionary, had been eaten in Fiji. I did not know, and still do not know, whether he was in earnest or pulling my leg as a naïve young man.

And then there was a chapter titled T*he Chameleon and the Sun-god Lisa on the West African Slave Coast.* This, I admit, might not get many pulses racing, but the opening sentence, 'It is a well-known fact that for most Africans the chameleon is a "peculiar" animal,' was for me a little like Proust's madeleine, for in East Africa where I worked the people believed that the bite of the chameleon was deadly poison and that if one got into your hair it would never get out. Probably more and worse than this was believed of it also, for I once caused a little platoon of soldiers to run away from me in terror into the bush because I approached them with a chameleon (for me a fascinating creature) in my hand. The paper in Marett's festschrift says that in the southern part of what used to be called Dahomey:

> When a pregnant woman, while walking in the bush, suddenly meets a chameleon and she gets frightened, the child which she delivers will be seized by the chameleon.

It is odd that people who have lived in close proximity to these harmless, if prehistoric-looking, creatures for thousands for years should have remained so superstitious about them, but I am much less disdainful of such error that I would once have been, for most of our minds are full of beliefs which are probably mistaken and for which we could give no evidence other than the authority from whom we first heard or read them.

But none of this would have induced me to buy the book had it not contained an essay entitled *Snobbery* by an anthropologist called A M Hocart. The latter was a very interesting man, a man of real substance, though hardly a household name. Like Merett a classicist, he was fluent in French and German, and learnt all the languages of the places in which he lived, as a schoolmaster, colonial administrator or researcher, from the language spoken by a tribe in the Solomon Islands, where he participated in the first anthropological field trip ever carried out, and

Fijian to Pali, the scriptural language of Theravada Buddhism. He never succeeded in obtaining an academic post in Britain, however, and was eventually appointed Professor of Sociology at Cairo University, dying there of a tropical infection contacted on a field trip. His books are more highly regarded nowadays than those of the man whose work he was celebrating in the festschrift, though perhaps titles such as *The Northern Fijian States* or *The Cult of the Dead in Eddystone of the Solomons* were never destined for the best-seller list.

The subject of his essay in the festschrift, *Snobbery*, seems to me one whose importance it underestimates, both in its practical and moral significance. I doubt that there is anyone completely free of this vice, either in its direct or inverted forms; this is because it is a basic human need, though not a human right, to feel superior to someone else.

Hocart's opening paragraphs are of a completely different readability from the rest of the book:

> The desire to emulate one's better has been a most potent, perhaps the most potent, force in the diffusion of customs. Yet it has received scarcely any notice from sociologists. Why?
>
> In the first place we are not honest with ourselves. Few like to admit that they adopt new ways because they want to rise to a higher social status or fear to drop to a lower one, in short that they are snobs. It is especially difficult to admit as much in these days of equalitarianism, when only low people admit they have betters, and it is part of the social rise to recognize no superiors.

This is acute and well-expressed; but since Hocart's day something rather peculiar has happened: there has been a reversal of the direction of the emulation. Until quite recently, emulators emulated those higher in the social scale than themselves, which meant of course that there were more emulators than emulated. Nowadays, however, it is persons in or from a higher social class who emulate those in a lower social class. They adopt the manner of speaking, dressing and cultural tastes of those below them. Intellectuals affect vulgar expressions and anyone with an avowed uninterest either in sport or in popular music is suspected at once of enmity towards the people, of the kind that at one time earned a ride in the *charrette* to the guillotine.

What does this change in the direction of cultural influence and aspiration signify? I think it signifies the complete ideological victory of egalitarianism, from which few dare derogate. Of course, there is a vast difference between the *pays idéologique* and the *pays réel*, that is to say between the way people think they ought to feel and act, and how they actually do feel and act. The desire for social and economic advance, to be at the top rather than at the bottom of the social scale, is as acute as ever. The scramble for position and prestige is ferocious. But the desire to stand out from and above one's fellows cannot be avowed even in the privacy of one's own skull, let alone in public—except perhaps in the context of sport, and there only because the common man accepts that sport can only entertain him where such competitiveness exists.

The downward cultural aspiration of those in the upper social echelons is purely defensive. If they indulge in egalitarianism in the symbolic field, they hope that their economic inegalitarianism will go, if not unnoticed, at least less noticed. They are all playing Marie Antoinette playing shepherdess. Once they are in private, they can drop their affected egalitarianism for public consumption and become what they are in reality, namely ferocious elitists. In other words, downward cultural aspiration, or apparent aspiration, is the means by which the contradiction between the *pays idéologique* is reconciled, though only in appearance, with the *pays réel.* And in a society in which what is virtual is as important as, if not more important than, what is real, an apparent reconciliation is as important as a real one.

The problem is that what starts as affectation becomes habit which becomes character. In the end, the play-acting becomes real. If Marie Antoinette had played shepherdess for long and often enough, that is what eventually she would have been. And so in the end the coarseness of popular culture triumphs over (by degrees, to be sure) all other forms.

If, as Hocart says, 'The desire to emulate one's better has been a most potent, perhaps the most potent, force in the diffusion of customs,' the fact that the higher echelons now ape the lower means that the lower have no need to aspire to anything in order to imagine themselves to be rising in the social scale, for there is nothing higher to emulate. This false egalitarianism serves, then, to conserve the social structure as a fly is conserved in amber. Social mobility falls while culture becomes less refined. There is therefore nothing to be said for this pretence, except perhaps that it dampens outrage against inequality.

'It has been the purpose of this paper,' concludes Hocart, 'to show that [snobbery] has played a very important part in the growth of civilization.' Perhaps so; but again we meet with a contradiction, for in individuals we almost always find it intensely disagreeable. Perhaps the best thing to be is a snob without showing it.

28
Reading Your Stasi

NOSTALGIA, that affection for the past that almost inevitably increases with age, is often derided as dangerous or reactionary because it is mistaken for a desire for a return to that past. This is a mistake: nostalgia is not a political programme and would not be nostalgia at all if it did not entail an awareness that the past cannot be returned to, that it is irrecoverable, that Time's arrow flies in one direction only, and that (to reverse the Leninist justification for the most frightful bestiality), you cannot make eggs out of an omelette. And the fact that many people excoriate nostalgia because they take it for a political programme demonstrates just how politicised our minds and souls have become, probably a consequence of the greatly increased size and influence of the state in our lives. It is true that nostalgia may serve to make us prudent or cautious, for it reminds us that loss is as possible as gain, and indeed is often inseparable from it; but it is not in itself an obstacle to progress, any more than it is a defence against deterioration. If one does not regret the past, one regrets one's life.

Of course nostalgia can easily attach to unworthy or even evil objects. Old Nazis, it is said, liked to meet and talk about the 'good old days,' the 'best' time of their lives. By best is meant the time that they most enjoyed, not the time in which they did most good or did least harm. At a much lower level of perversity, one may be nostalgic for things that one would certainly not want to go back to, such as the food of one's childhood or the classroom of a bad teacher. Nostalgia seems to have its own laws that are not those of everyday judgment.

I say this because I have a nostalgia for something that I detested at the time and detest still, namely communism as it was practised in Eastern Europe. I have not gone soft in the head, nor changed my opinion of it; but I sometimes wished it was still there so that I could experience the thrill of crossing the Iron Curtain. I recognise that this is an entirely self-indulgent wish, for it pits my enjoyment of a relatively fleeting sensation against the prolonged suffering of millions of people: I certainly wouldn't act upon it, but what is so is so and the thoughts that run through my mind run through my mind.

The last lines of Cavafy's famous poem, Waiting for the Barbarians, run:

> And now, what's going to happen to us without barbarians?
> They were, those people, a kind of solution.

Communists were also a kind of solution for us for many years; the world they created was something near, bordering and threatening us, that was worse, far worse, than anything that we had, no matter what our dissatisfactions with what we had might have been. When this something was snatched from us by its unexpected collapse, we were left with our dissatisfactions naked and unadorned, as it were, without the consolation for them that the existence of communism not very far away offered us. The communists simplified the world for us, in the way that a man whose life is threatened does not worry about what he is going to have for dinner, or what colour to paint his study.

But in my case there is something much more personal, less abstract and philosophical, to my nostalgia for the days of the Iron Curtain than that. I miss the atmosphere of the communist days: the dim lights, the unanimated streets, the absence of traffic, the smell of bad, adulterated fuel that polluted the air, the hushed voices, the echoing footfall, the grey dilapidation, the feeling of satisfaction if one found anything to eat, and above all the frisson of fear that one was being watched and followed. For a young man such as I—with an easy escape route, of course, for I do not pretend that my experience had anything to do, or bore any comparison with, that of the people actually living in those countries—the idea that I might be considered dangerous enough to be watched or followed was flattering, for in my own country I was of no account whatsoever. And then, on the very brief occasions when one made human contact with someone in those benighted, oppressed lands, that were like flashes of lightning that illuminated for a second a black landscape, one sensed a person with an intensity of experience much deeper than one's own, a person who lived on a philosophical plane, whose life had been stripped down to the essential: and whom, with foolish romanticism, one almost envied. What did I have to set against their problems: an unhappy childhood, uncertainty about my career? Mere trifles by comparison with the *peine forte et dure* that was life in the Peoples' Republics, most of which I visited, incidentally, when their more sanguinary phase was over, although not beyond possibility of resuscitation.

Needless to say, my enjoyment of trips behind the Iron Curtain was not really much different from that of people who enjoy the Chamber of Horrors in Madame Tussaud's waxworks, where they thrill to the figures and accoutrements of notorious murderers without in the least wishing to be murdered themselves. My enjoyment behind the Iron Curtain was salacious, prurient and self-indulgent, with just enough of a grain of philosophy thrown in to assure myself that I had a higher purpose in thus enjoying myself.

So I do not claim for my nostalgia any superior sensibility, much less a proper role in political thought or philosophy. In fact, I am rather ashamed of it, that I am capable of looking back on what was a terrible period for millions with something like affection. But so it is: the heart has its reasons that reason knows not of. And all my nostalgia (which is infrequent, I do not want to give the impression that it plays an important part in my life, or that I was at the time anything other than a convinced Cold Warrior) returned in force when I happened upon a memoir of life in East Germany—one of only two communist states, unless you count Mongolia, Sao Tomé e Principe, Guinea Bissau and Cabo Verde, that I never visited—titled *Red Love: the Story of an East German Family*, by a German journalist and newspaper editor called Maxim Leo.

Born in 1970, the author had 19 years of living in a workers' paradise and then quickly made his way in the new conditions of freedom, which he came with equal speed to consider normal, as if tyranny were somehow unnatural. (I remember being impressed by young people in Ceausescu's Romania who told me that, though they had known nothing else, they knew that how they were living in Romania was not normal.) But Maxim Leo's memoir is not a mere propagandistic paean of praise to liberty as we know it—or perhaps I should say as we once knew it, since it seems to be eroding like a cliff before repeated strong tides. Rather, it is a subtle exploration of the contorted psychology induced by totalitarianism. For it should go without saying than no regime can survive evoking only uncompromising opposition: it must have some supporters, and appeal to the interests of a proportion of the population.

The author's maternal grandfather was a rich lawyer who had fallen foul of Goebbels in the early 20s by representing a French general who sued Goebbels for libel when Goebbels accused him of having caused his limp by torturing him as a prisoner. The author's grandfather won the General's case by proving that Goebbels had been born with a club-foot and had been exempted from military service because of it. When the Nazis came to power, the grandfather was beaten severely and spent some time in a concentration camp. Not only had Goebbels not forgotten, but the grandfather was of part Jewish descent though he was not Jewish.

He and the author's father, then a boy, fled to France. The boy became as French as he was German; he also decided to be a communist, on the not uncommon but nonetheless erroneous view that one's enemy's enemy is one's friend. (This was well before the Ribbentrop-Molotov Pact.) When war came, the author's father fled to the unoccupied zone and joined the resistance, to whom, as bilingual in German and French, he was extremely useful, and in whose service he was extremely brave. The account of his life in the resistance reads so excitingly that it is difficult to believe that it is true: but it is. Having survived—just—it would have been difficult for the rest of his life not to have been an anti-climax.

In addition, he had by then become a dogmatic communist—like the other members of the resistance with whom he had fought. Eventually he returned to East Germany and led a privileged existence as a journalist and spy for the regime, though he had his secret reservations. He passed on his communist convictions to his daughter, the author's mother, who found it increasingly difficult to reconcile them with the reality around her, but remained fundamentally loyal to the regime until five minutes to midnight.

The author's paternal grandfather, whom he did not get to know until late in his life (he had deserted the author's grandmother before he was born), became a loyal supporter of the regime by a different route. An enthusiastic Nazi and soldier until a week before the surrender, he found a new cause in the German Democratic Republic as a teacher and headmaster, and prospered, at least by local standards. According to the author, he would have been a convinced believer in any system under which he happened to find himself: and perhaps most of mankind is like that.

His son, with whom he had no contact, was a loyal rebel, if I may so put it. He was an artist leading a mildly double life: as the Stasi file on him put it, he was questioning of the regime but not hostile to it. When the destruction of the Wall came he was disorientated: he felt he had nothing any longer to be against, none of his little gestures counted for anything. He became insignificant, therefore, and rather movingly made a decision not to join in the unleashed scramble for material goods, preferring to live as if in Van Gogh's bedroom, with a chair, a table and a bedstead, and nothing else.

The author conveys very well the mental contortions required to live in East Germany (or in any such regime): the mixture of belief, cynicism, indifference, calculation, compromise, wilful ignorance, opportunism, bravery, effrontery and all the many shades and interactions between them. The author does not make himself out a hero, quite the reverse: he is an ordinary, intelligent likeable person who just wants a 'normal' life and would prefer to live without overt political interference.

The moral reprehensibility and degradation of the regime was obvious both from the outside and in retrospect: but from within and at the time, matters were often more equivocal. Perhaps the hardest words in the book are reserved for those in the west who admired the GDR—different from the attitude of François Mauriac, who famously said that he liked Germany so much that he was glad there were two of them. In 1987, when it still looked as if the GDR might last for ever, the author's maternal grandfather, taking advantage of his political position, took the author on a trip to France, an enormous privilege for that time and from that place. Together, they visited political allies in France, mainly rich intellectuals. Having lunch in the luxurious villa in the South of France of one of those intellectuals, the young Maxim wonders 'How you can sit in a villa like that and rave about the GDR?' He then says, 'I reflect that it's a very pleasant business, being a revolutionary in the South of France.'

The previous owner of the book has marked these two sentences with a green pen, the only ones he had so marked. Obviously he thought they were of particular significance: I think he was right. No one is as self-destructive in the name of generosity of spirit as the fortunate man.

29
Sir Joshua and the Tumbling Walls

THE ASSOCIATION of ideas is itself an idea that has fallen into comparative desuetude of late because of its supposed lack of explanatory power, but it still seems to me useful as a way of describing how one idea evokes another. Certainly I seem very rarely to read a book nowadays without it calling forth in my mind memories or other kinds of associations: perhaps this is merely testimony to the length of my life, or alternatively to my choice of reading matter.

When I picked up a book, then, of Sir Joshua Reynolds' previously unpublished writings (previous, that is, to 1952), I thought back to my days as a student when I attended a lecture by a (then) famous art historian, whose name I shall protect from obloquy by not mentioning it, in which he said that Reynolds was a shallow, vulgar painter, a remark that struck me, despite the prissy fastidious curl of the lip with which it was delivered, as itself rather shallow and vulgar. I am an admirer of Reynolds both as a painter and a man; and at their best his portraits penetrated the complex and deep character of their subjects. His portraits of Samuel Johnson, for example, whom he loved and admired above all men, are reverent without flattery. He does not try to make Johnson a handsome man, but he makes him what he was, a remarkable one. If Reynolds did not work always at his best (he was, after all, very prolific), I remember Somerset Maugham's dictum that only a very mediocre writer is always at his best.

In this book, *Portraits*, Reynolds shows that it was no accident that his portraits penetrated the character as well as they represented the physical appearance of his sitters. The book contains three character sketches in words of three of the great men of his time, Oliver Goldsmith, Doctor Johnson and David Garrick. These character sketches were not intended for publication, that of Doctor Johnson having been for the private use of James Boswell in writing his great *Life*; but though never revised, they are still worth reading because Reynolds had caught the habit of writing and thinking well from Johnson himself, at whose feet he had sat and of whom he wrote, very acutely:

> Another circumstance... contributed not a little to the powers which he had of expressing himself, which was a rule... of always on every occasion speaking his best, whether the person to whom he addressed himself was or was not capable of comprehending him... Dr. Johnson, by this continued practice, made that a habit which was at first an exertion...

When a young philosopher asked me how he could learn to write clearly, I told him to develop the habit of thinking in aphorisms.

One of the most remarkable things about Reynolds' character sketch of Johnson is the clarity with which he draws attention to his great friend's faults and defects. Among them were rudeness (tempered by a readiness to apologise) and a tendency 'to entertain prejudices on very slight foundation, giving an opinion perhaps first at random, but from its being contradicted he thinks himself obliged always stubbornly to support—or if he could not support, still not to acquiesce.' This is a fault which I have myself, and perhaps is more commonly distributed than its opposite virtues, an unwillingness to express an opinion when ignorant of the subject, and a corresponding willingness to accept correction in the light of further facts and logic. I suspect, however, that a man who had those virtues to the very highest degree would never find his Boswell, nor need him. It is perhaps fortunate that there are more talkers for victory than for truth, or else conversation would be mostly silenced.

'You will wonder,' writes Reynolds, 'to hear a person who loved him so sincerely speak thus freely of his friend, but you must recollect I am not writing his panegyric, but as if on oath not only to give the truth but the whole truth.' Is this not admirable? The praise of such a man is worth that of a thousand hagiographers or a million flatterers.

Reynolds knew the actor of European celebrity, David Garrick, well, but did not like him, even though he had great charm. And Reynolds had the capacity to damn succinctly:

> Great as Garrick was on the stage, he was at least equal if not superior at the table [at a dinner party], and here he had too much the same habit of preparing himself, as if he was to act a principal part.

In other words, he was never truly himself, there was no self to be true to.

Garrick's greatest fault—and Reynolds' words carry the conviction of a man who was not only perceptive but unusually honest—was his avidity for fame and superficial triumph. When he went into company he arranged always to be called out as if he were wanted somewhere else, just to create an impression of being important and in demand; and Reynolds' remarks on the vanity of celebrity are more than ever apt when in an age when for many it is the only thing worth having:

> Garrick… died without a friend; so did Lord Chesterfield. The moral to be drawn from their lives is this: that this passion for fame, however proper when within due bounds as a link in the social chain, as a spur to our exertions to acquire and deserve the affections of our brethren, yet when this passion is carried to excess, like every other excess it becomes a vice, either ridiculous, or odious, or sometimes criminal. An inordinate desire for fame produces an entire neglect of their old friends, or we may rather say they never have any friends; their whole desire and ambition is centred in extending their reputation by showing their tricks before fresh new men. That moment you begin to congratulate yourself on your new acquaintance, your intimacy ceases. A worse consequence: by degrees all the principles of right and wrong, whatever dignifies human nature, is lost, or not attended to when in competition with the shadow of fame. They begin to grow short-sighted and seize with such greediness the immediate gratification that they forfeit every title to what is truly praiseworthy, steadiness of conduct. From having no general principle they live in perpetual anxiety what conduct to take on every occasion to insure this petty praise.

Perhaps this explains the propensity of modern celebrities to adopt political causes: they are in search of the 'general principle' that Reynolds says that they lack; but by adopting such a cause (always one that puts them on the side of the unthinking angels) they find a 'general principle' without having to change their conduct. Indeed, with proper public relation, they can make the cause they adopt serve their fame.

I read Reynolds' character sketch of Oliver Goldsmith with a degree of dismay and even pain, for Goldsmith's abiding vice (he had many virtues also) reminded me forcefully of my father.

> It must be confessed—wrote Reynolds—that whoever excelled in any art or science, however remote from [Goldsmith's] own, was sure to be considered by him as a rival. It was sufficient that he was an object of praise, as if he thought that the world had but a certain quantity of that commodity to give away, and what was bestowed upon others made less come to his share.

That was an exact depiction of my father's jealousy of praise, with the result that I never heard him unreservedly praise anyone (with the exception of his teachers fifty, sixty, or seventy years earlier); what started as praise in his mouth ended up as adverse criticism, so many qualification and derogations did he append. This inability to praise others sincerely or unreservedly was, in fact, an obstacle to the achievements which his great gifts might otherwise have led: for so great was his jealousy of praise that I think that he could not properly recognise the merits of others even in the privacy of his own mind. This meant that he could not co-operate with gifted, intelligent or worthy men: and such co-operation is necessary to success because no man is an island. I learnt from my father, what he never intended me to learn, that character was at least as important in success as ability.

Goldsmith's attempted hoarding of praise unto himself, however, was counteracted by his virtues. Of it, Reynolds—himself a very tolerant man—said:

> It was so far from being of that black malignant kind which excites hatred and disgust that it was, from being so artless and obvious, only ridiculous.

It astonished me how the off-scourings of Reynolds' pen could be of such contemporary relevance. There is a previously unpublished essay in the book, an ironical discourse on art, that I would distribute by the thousand in the art schools of the west, whose main purpose, it seems to me, is to corrupt youth, or that pert of it with artistic leanings. Perhaps, in distributing it, it would be advisable to attach a commentary to it, for what Sir Joshua was satirising were the very attitudes and beliefs that have become an orthodoxy in the world of art-schools. Here is a little bit of Sir Joshua's satire:

> Genius, as it disdains all assistance, so it defies all obstacles. The student here may inform himself whether he has been favoured by heaven with this truly divine gift. If he finds it necessary to copy, to study the works of other painters, or any way to seek for help for himself, he may be sure that he has received nothing of that inspiration… Let the student consider with himself whether he is impelled forward by irresistible instinct. He himself is little more than a machine, unconscious of the power which impels him forward to the instant performance of what others learn by the slow methods of rules and precepts.

Reynolds could have been writing of present-day art schools. His next words are as if engraved over their entrance, as the injunction to know thyself was inscribed at the entrance to the Delphic Temple of Apollo:

> What is the use of rules, but to cramp and fetter genius?

Reynolds continues:

> The rules which dull men have introduced into liberal arts smother that flame which would otherwise blaze out in originality of invention.

This is the attitude of the art schools to a T, which imbue their students with the gratifying notion that originality unhindered by the weight or chains of the past is the highest goal at which they can aim, in the achievement of which ignorance will be a positive aid to them, and which explains why the exhibits in the graduating exhibitions of modern art schools almost always resemble the productions of kindergartens: rare is the talent that can survive an art school education, if education rather than indoctrination is what it deserves to be called. In satirising the romantic notion of untutored genius, Sir Joshua proved himself prescient; and he would not have been surprised by the results when art schools took his satire not as a warning but as a blueprint.

In his *Sixth Discourse*, Sir Joshua wrote:

> To derive all from native power, to owe nothing to another, is the praise which men who do not much think on what they are saying bestow upon others, and sometimes on themselves: and their imaginary dignity is heightened by a supercilious censure of the low, the barren, the grovelling, the servile imitator.

It would be no surprise, he continued, if the student, 'frightened by these terrific and disgraceful epithets, should let fall his pencil... and consider it as hopeless to set about acquiring by the imitation of any human master what he is taught to suppose is a matter of inspiration from heaven.'

Reynolds diagnosed, if he did not foresee, the sickness of much of the modern aesthetic (if aesthetic is quite the word for it). He knew that, if even Homer nodded, even Mozart laboured.

30
Hazards of Hazlitt

ON A CROWDED train a few days ago I was reading Hazlitt preparatory to writing an essay comparing his Shakespeare criticism with that of Dr Johnson (whom he detested). Which of them was the more acute, the more penetrating? And the essay which I happened to read on the train was *On the Ignorance of the Learned*, which ends with the famous words:

> If we wish to know the force of human genius we should read Shakespeare. If we wish to know the insignificance of human learning we may study his commentators.

As Hazlitt had by then written his book about Shakespeare's characters, he presumably knew whereof he spoke.

The essay both delighted and irritated me. Delighted irritation is, of course, a very pleasant state of mind, for it combines the enjoyments of moral outrage with those of aesthetic appreciation. In a matter of only a few pages I found myself veering, staggering perhaps, between joyous agreement and the deepest exasperation. This, perhaps, is not surprising because I am one of those strange but by no means uncommon creatures, an anti-intellectual intellectual—as, indeed, was Hazlitt.

When I read—or rather re-read, for I had read the essay more than once before—the affirmation that 'There is no dogma, however fierce or foolish, to which these persons [the learned] have not set their seals, and tried to impose on the understandings of their followers…' I nodded vigorously and enthusiastically, and let out an explosive little 'Ha!,' to the evident discomfort of those sitting next or opposite to me, who thought I might be mad. Or again: 'They see things not as they are, but as they find them in books, and "wink and shut their apprehensions up," in order that they may discover nothing to interfere with their prejudices or convince them of their absurdity.' One cannot help but think when reading this passage how apposite it is to all those intellectuals of the twentieth century who lined up to extol regimes such as Stalin's, Mao's or even (in fewer cases) Pol Pot's. One also thinks of Cicero's remark, nearly two millennia before, that there was nothing so absurd that some philosopher has not said it, and Orwell's nearly a century and a half later, that there are some things so absurd that only an intellectual could believe them. Nothing changes.

And yet this is all a little sweeping. It usually takes a philosopher to know that what a philosopher has said is absurd. Not every intellectual believes six impossible things before breakfast, and furthermore it often requires intellectuals to undo the harm that other intellectuals do. No one would deny Raymond Aron, for example, the name of intellectual merely because he failed to believe and opposed the lies and equivocations of Jean-Paul Sartre. From the fact that intellectuals have believed absurdities, it does not follow either that, *ex officio*, they believe only absurdities, or that only intellectuals believe absurdities. Orwell, the patron saint of everyone who wants to claim him as such, was not speaking the literal truth when he said that some things are so absurd that only intellectuals could believe them; rather he was trying to destroy blind faith in the superior wisdom of intellectuals (prevalent mainly among themselves). No one who surveys human history, however superficially, could possibly come to the conclusion that the common people were incapable of the utmost credulity, or that such credulity can be defeated once and for all and will never arise among them again. And there is a further complication since the time of Cicero, Hazlitt and Orwell: the class of person who considers himself an intellectual has expanded out of all recognition, making generalisation even more difficult and hazardous. Still, an anti-intellectual intellectual such as I cannot but question whether an increase in the number of persons who consider themselves intellectuals, or merely intellectual, is altogether a good thing.

Notwithstanding my statistical reservations, Hazlitt's words have contemporary resonance. When he says that there is no doctrine, however fierce or foolish, that the learned have not tried to impose on the understanding of their followers, who would not think (in our day) of Moslem intellectuals who promote their murderous absurdities? They are often, in their way, learned men; but it would have been far better for them to have known and thought nothing than to have known and thought what they have known and thought. One can, after all, be learned in the productions of astrologers or alchemists without knowing anything worth knowing. No doubt such productions are matters of interest to specialist historians of certain epochs, but they are no guides to modern life. Alas, we are now in the position of having to concern ourselves with a fierce and foolish doctrine, of no intrinsic intellectual interest whatever (much less than that of, say, Marxism), merely because some of the learned, in Hazlitt's derogatory sense, have tried, with some practical success, 'to impose it on the understandings of their followers.'

But Hazlitt goes too far—an occupational hazard of intellectuals who want to attract and keep an audience or readership. Moderation is rarely interesting, but there is no reason, as Bertrand Russell once said, why the truth when found should be interesting. So Hazlitt says that if the learned are ignorant, the ignorant are learned. This is preposterous.

In the first place, Hazlitt loads his dialectical dice by equating learning with pedantry, the learned with the kind of people who can turn ancient Greek verse into Latin epigram without themselves ever having an original thought. He says that such people are often incapable of the simplest practical tasks and are narrow in their outlook and interests. They know nothing of art, music or science, but account themselves superior to all those who are not like them. They call 'mechanical' all accomplishments that do not relate to their own particular, tiny and useless skill.

It is true that learning and pedantry sometimes go together, but by no means are all the learned pedantic (the most learned people I have known personally have been accomplished in several different fields, including practical ones unrelated to their own), while the unlearned are not always immune from pedantry. When reviewing a book about a subject of which I know little or nothing, for example, I delight to come across an error which I can recognise. There is more rejoicing in the heart of a pedant over one mistake than over ninety-nine facts he didn't know. I have quite a number of old books in which a previous reader has marked with an underlining or by an exclamation mark in the margin the only typographical error in the whole volume. It is as if that reader had been reading only in the hope of finding such an error, so that, being a frustrated intellectual himself, he could feel superior to the author of the book he was reading.

But the identification of learning with pedantry is not Hazlitt's only mistake. He is a populist in the worst sense. He says, for example, the 'you will hear more good things on the outside of a stage-coach from London to Oxford than if you were to pass a twelvemonth with the undergraduates, or heads of colleges, of that university.' Times may have changed, but I took a little time off from reading to listen to the three men from Liverpool next to me who were talking among themselves. What were the good things they said? They had but two subjects: the price of various kinds of beer in various kinds of bars, and the selection of the Liverpool football team (the former manager of which once said that football was not a matter of life and death—it was much more important than that). I suspect that I could have spent a twelvemonth in the company of these men and heard of little but beer and football. This does not mean that they were bad men, but it would rather cast doubt on their superior wit.

But it is not only superior wit with which the common, unlearned people are endowed in Hazlitt's opinion, but superior wisdom. This is what he says:

> Above all the mass of society have common sense, which the learned in all ages want. The vulgar are in the right when they judge for themselves; they are wrong when they trust to their blind guides.

Now it is true that there are some absurd doctrines propounded by the learned which the 'mass of society' does not come to believe, but is it common sense that protects them, or their lack of understanding or interest? After all, they are perfectly capable of believing many absurdities. And if they are endowed with common sense *ex officio*, how comes it that 'they trust to their blind guides'?

Hazlitt goes on to say:

> The celebrated nonconformist divine, Baxter, was almost stoned to death by the good women of Kidderminster for asserting from the pulpit that "hell was paved with infants' skulls"; but, by force of argument, and of learned quotations from the Fathers, the reverend preacher at length prevailed over the scruples of his congregation, and over reason and humanity.

Now this passage has a special personal interest for me because, when I am in England, I live next door but four to a house on whose frontage are inscribed the words, *In this house lived the learned and eloquent Richard Baxter 1640-41*, which for some reason I read for a number of years as 'learned and elegant,' perhaps because I prefer elegance to eloquence, the latter being possible in the service of a very bad cause.

But let us return to Hazlitt. Is nearly stoning a preacher to death a sign of the female congregation's common sense that he extols? Common sense, surely, would laugh at the doctrine Baxter propounded (if, that is, Hazlitt's representation of it is correct). And if the common sense of the populace were so powerful a shield against Baxter's 'fierce and foolish doctrine,' how came it that he was able to prove, by quotation from supposed authorities, that the road to hell really was paved with babies' skulls? It is difficult not to conclude that the proper defence against Baxter's horrible proposition was common sense allied with learning and eloquence. In other words, common sense is necessary but not sufficient.

Hazlitt pays tribute to women, but not of a kind to please modern feminists. Women, he says, 'have often more of what is called good sense than men… They cannot reason wrong; for they do not reason at all.' Quite apart from displeasing modern women, this is a dangerous form of irrationalism; for if it is true that mankind cannot live by reason alone, it is also true that it cannot live without it. And when Hazlitt goes on to say that 'uneducated people have the most exuberance of invention and the greatest freedom from prejudice,' he displays only his lack of acquaintance with humanity. This is proved by his further assertion that Shakespeare was such an uneducated person. Shakespeare was uneducated (at worst) only in *le tout Paris* sense of the world, a deeply snobbish sense.

But why should Hazlitt have been so eager to claim virtues for the common people when what he says demonstrates a rather limited or selective acquaintance with them? I think he is thereby trying to prove his political virtue, a very modern thing to try to do. *Vox populi, vox dei.* Harm, including bad taste, therefore comes only from the learned, from the rich, from the educated, from the higher reaches of society, from the authorities, but for whom life would be much better than it is. There is no essential flaw or contradiction in human nature; and so it is not possible to think that both the learned and the unlearned can be ignorant, wicked or foolish, each in their own way, because the attractions of error and evil are always present and often great. The common people must be intrinsically good if life is to be perfectible. The ignorance of the learned is Hazlitt's answer to the problem of evil.

31
From Scotland to Timor

ONCE YOU HAVE reached a certain age and experienced the majority of all that you will ever experience, almost everything reminds you of something else. It is as if the world were full of *double entendres* in which nothing meant only what it appeared to mean. The association of ideas becomes so strong that the past becomes almost as real and living as the present: you experience two realities simultaneously. This is pleasurable and is one of the compensations of age. It deepens and enriches life.

The other day I happened to be re-reading a favourite story of mine, Robert Louis Stevenson's *The Body Snatcher*. One of the reasons, no doubt bad, that it is a favourite of mine is that I think that I discovered the identity of one of the main characters in it. Not being any kind of scholar, let alone that of the life and works of RLS, I cannot be sure that my discovery was original rather than a rediscovery of what was already well-known: an overestimation of one's originality being the occupational hazard of the unlearned.

The story begins in the inn of a tiny Scottish settlement called Debenham. Four of the locals are sitting drinking, one of them the narrator and another a man called Fettes who studied medicine at Edinburgh University but never practised medicine. A local landowner and Member of Parliament has been struck down by apoplexy *en route* for London, from which his very grand and important doctor has been summoned to treat him. He arrives.

The great man is called Wolfe Macfarlane, and he was a close acquaintance earlier in life of Fettes, whom he is far from pleased to meet again. Now this Macfarlane, at least according to me, is clearly Sir William Fergusson, surgeon to Queen Victoria, who died seven years before the story was published. Stevenson would never have dared publish it, even had he written it, before Fergusson's death.

In the story which unfolds, Macfarlane was in earlier years teaching assistant to an anatomist in Edinburgh named in the story simply as K. In those days, before the Anatomy Act of 1832, the only legal source of bodies for dissection by surgeons and anatomists in Britain was that of hanged criminals. Indeed, so hated was dissection of the human body at the time that to be condemned to be anatomised after execution by hanging was regarded as almost the worse part of the punishment.

The shortage of bodies for dissection was rectified by body-snatchers, men who dug up the freshly-interred and delivered them (at a high price) to the anatomy schools such as K's. It was profitable for all concerned, for the anatomy schools were also private institutions that charged students for the privilege of dissecting.

Again according to the story, Macfarlane, whose duties at the time included accepting and paying for bodies for dissection on behalf of K, knew perfectly well that some of the bodies were of people murdered specially for the purpose. One of the delivered bodies was of a young woman well-known on the streets of Edinburgh who had been seen alive and well on the very day before her delivery to the anatomy school as a corpse. Macfarlane knows perfectly well that she has not died of natural causes but says nothing: once she is dissected no one will be any the wiser. He is completely without scruple.

This is a retelling of the history of Burke and Hare, who extended body-snatching to murder in order to supply the famous (and soon to be infamous) anatomy school of Dr Robert Knox—the K of the story. Knox was suspected all along of having known that some of the bodies sold to his school for dissection were murdered, not body-snatched from the grave. He had to flee the city, his activities and those of his suppliers giving rise to a children's ditty:

> Up the close and down the stair,
> In the house with Burke and Hare.
> Burke's the butcher, Hare's the thief,
> Knox, the boy who buys the beef.

Now Dr Knox's assistant at the time was one William Fergusson, who a little later in life moved, just as Dr Macfarlane did in the story, from Edinburgh to London, where he became a famous surgeon knighted and appointed to the household of Queen Victoria. According to his obituaries, Fergusson's personality was exactly as Macfarlane's is described in the story. A short biography of Fergusson was published in 1961 in the journal *Medical History*, written by another very distinguished surgeon, Sir Gordon Gordon-Taylor:

> William Fergusson became a pupil of Robert Knox who appointed him a demonstrator in 1828 at the early age of 20… just after Fergusson joined him, the period of the 'Burke and Hare' affair [began], when it transpired that 16 people had been murdered for the sale of their bodies to unwitting anatomical teachers.

But were they really unwitting? Gordon-Taylor absolves Fergusson by quoting William Burke's confession before he was hanged:

> That worthy gentleman, Mr Fergusson, was the only man that ever questioned me about the bodies. He inquired where we got that young woman. Mary Paterson, because she would seem to have been well known to the students.

This does not seem to me very strong evidence of innocence, and could just as well be used against Fergusson. Stevenson in effect accused Fergusson of having been an accessory to murder, indeed an accessory to serial murder, and in so doing was pulling down a pillar of Victorian respectability.

But the association of Wolfe Macfarlane with Sir William Fergusson was not the one that I made as I re-read the story this time. It took me back instead to my brief time in East Timor during the Indonesian occupation of that unhappy land. I was there to help in the making of a clandestine film about the atrocities committed by the Indonesians with the blessing, and even the actual connivance, of western powers. The Indonesians were favoured because they were firmly anti-communist and East Timor was a former Portuguese colony. Former Portuguese colonies had an unfortunate propensity (unfortunate for their populations as well as for the western powers) of turning communist. The strange thing was that the Indonesians had succeeded in creating an atmosphere in the capital city, Dili, that was almost East European. The pall of tyranny hung over it as if it were Prague circa 1954; the deadness in the streets was extraordinary. It turned the tropics grey.

The pretence of the Indonesians at the time was that its occupation of that part of the island of Timor was perfectly legal and that everything was proceeding normally. The East Timorese, according to them, welcome the opportunity to be part of Indonesia. They therefore had no pretext for keeping foreigners out, though very few indeed wanted to go, thanks to the stories of massacre that emerged intermittently from the island. The Indonesians were imposing their language on the territory and it was illegal there to speak Portuguese: an overheard word of that language could get you disappeared for good, especially if you were Timorese. I had come to interview a dissident in the capital, whom I interviewed in that dangerous language which I do not speak at all well, but on which I had brushed up a little at the time. I had a video camera with me, an implement that I wielded even worse than I spoke Portuguese, and smuggling it round the island was distinctly dangerous. One of my few appearances on the silver screen, then, has been as a voice asking questions in bad Portuguese.

One of the more extraordinary experiences of my life was being serenaded in the best hotel in the capital by drunken Indonesian army officers who, like me, were staying there. Every evening they had a karaoke session in the bar, after a hard day's oppression. I was the only other guest in the hotel, and one of the officers, drunk, would approach me to ask me whether he could sing a song for me. It was, I suppose, a mark of friendliness of a kind, but one that I could have done without, first because I have a horror of karaoke as a genre and second, and more importantly, because I did not wish to be befriended by officers of an army rightly accused of many massacres and much cruelty. Luckily, difficulties in communication prevented me from having to choose a song from the officers' limited repertoire; they favoured songs of the most saccharine sentimentality. Ever since, I have associated such sentimentality with the worst kind of brutality and bad conscience.

One of the reasons, perhaps, why I got away with it all was that I made much of the fact that I was a doctor. Indeed, that was my pretext for entering the territory in the first place: I was supposed to be producing a report on conditions for a medical charity that was going to provide help to the population. The Indonesian authorities, on the pretence East Timor was now fully integrated into Indonesia, could not very well refuse a fact-finding mission without giving the game away.

When I arrived in villages, the news that a doctor had come spread very quickly and before long a great queue of people formed to consult me. Tuberculosis and other diseases were rampant, but of course there was little I could do. Medicines were in short supply and auxiliary assistance non-existent. However, if there is one faith that unites mankind it is faith in medicine, and the mere fact of having been examined, however briefly, by a doctor no doubt raised the spirits of many of the people who queues. Perhaps it helped to relieve the monotony of an existence in which the boredom of subsistence farming was normally relieved only by terror of the occupying force. It helped also to throw the Indonesian authorities off the scent.

Now, you may ask, how and in what way did *The Body Snatcher* put you in mind of East Timor, and all the memories that you have of it? Well, in the story Wolfe Macfarlane is called all the way from London to attend the local landowner and Member of Parliament who has had apoplexy (a stroke). Given the means of treatment available to the great doctor, his journey would have been a complete waste of time and effort; there was nothing he could have done for the patient. Indeed, the chances are that there would not be much he could have done in these circumstances even today. Macfarlane would have known his uselessness even before he set out, but it would have faltered his self-importance; to have refused the call on the grounds of impotence would have exposed his pretensions to greatness.

When I was just about to leave Dili for the much greener pastures of Bali, where I had arranged to meet my wife for a short holiday before travelling across the Pacific, I was asked to go to a Chinese merchant's house. The capital was a small enough place, and visitors so few, that the presence and profession of someone like me would have become common knowledge in no time.

The merchant, I was told, was very ill. Would I accept to attend him?

I went. When I reached his house, luxurious in the sense of being spacious but bare of those many electrical and electronic appurtenances that (falsely) we believe necessary for a decent existence, I found him deeply unconscious on his bed. He had clearly had a catastrophic stroke—apoplexy, in the language of *The Body Snatcher*. I was in the same situation as Wolfe Macfarlane, important but impotent. I thought the man would die, but his family, who were watching me from around the bed, were desperate that something should be done. He was a rich man, possibly the richest in the city and territory, and clearly there was no point in being such if nothing could be done for him. There was no hospital in East Timor, but there was one in Kupang, the capital of West Timor. I advised the anxious family to take him there. They put him in a pick-up truck and prepared to take him by rough roads to the metropolis of the island. It was evidently important to the family that every straw had been clutched at.

Of course, the Indonesians—by which I meant, essentially, the Javanese, who were in charge of the archipelago country—had no particular love for the Chinese, to put it mildly. But I trusted that even in these circumstances medical ethics would triumph, and my unknown colleagues would do their best for the stricken merchant, though it would almost certainly be of no avail.

And that is how, by reading RLS's *The Body Snatcher*, I was transported ten thousand miles in my imagination.

32
Traviata Trivia

A FEW NIGHTS AGO I went to the opera, or rather to the local cinema in which the opera was relayed live. It was *La Traviata* from the English National Opera company.

For some reason, which is, perhaps, not difficult to fathom, directors of operas these days feel the need to make their mark by innovative productions, for example by setting *Così fan tutte* on the Moon, or *The Flying Dutchman* on Lake Titicaca, or *The Barber of Seville* in Nazi Germany. But of course they particularly like settings in the present, preferably in rather down-at-heel or dispiriting environs, to remind us that the opera, all appearances to the contrary notwithstanding, is of the deepest (which means radical) contemporary political significance, and was intended as such. And their view of the present, to judge by the scenery and costumes, is a somewhat dismal one, for elegance or refinement of appearance or behaviour is rigorously excluded. In Victorian times, one was supposed not to frighten the horses; these days one mustn't frighten the proles.

Now this *Traviata* was sung in English which, notwithstanding the linguistic patriot that I am, is a language ill-suited to Verdi, though in many, perhaps even in most, other respects it is a marvellously flexible tongue. There was no point in singing it in English either, because subtitles or supertitles were still deemed necessary. Thus was achieved the worst of all worlds.

But that was the least of it. I don't mind a simple stage set, but I could not make out why Violetta and Alfredo kept trying to draw curtains across the stage and then draw them back again. This, I suppose, was the director's idea of *Symbolism*, but unfortunately it was difficult to work out what was symbolised, and you can't really have symbols without something being symbolised, otherwise it is like roast beef without the beef. Perhaps all those curtains symbolised the difference between appearance and reality, but again perhaps not. It is not true that every mystery is interesting.

But this, again, is a minor cavil. Poor Alfredo, whose singing was adequate, was about as far removed from a romantic hero as it is possible to imagine. He was short and by no means slender, and had something nerdy about him. None of this was his fault, of course, but it did not help to dress him up in a thick fawn-coloured cardigan and brown corduroy trousers and also allow, or require, him to wear thick-rimmed glasses (I expected carpet slippers to make their appearance, but they didn't). He looked more like a junior librarian in a small municipal library than a poet entering the fervidly luxurious demi-monde.

Violetta, Elizabeth Zharoff, was splendid if somewhat lacking in subtlety, but in a way it was unfortunate that she was so beautiful, for these days opera audiences demand proper acting with some semblance of plausibility. I remember the days when opera singers would make only perfunctory gestures in the direction of acting, and generally remained more or less rooted to the spot in costumes and sets of varying degrees of absurdity. They usually moved if they moved at all—or perhaps I should say sailed across choppy waters—like Dreadnoughts before the First World War. This had the great advantage of stimulating the audience's willing suspension of disbelief, because it was very necessary to suspend it, but nowadays, alas, audiences are more literal-minded and, in a sense, discriminating. And it was not remotely plausible that Violetta would fall in love with such an Alfredo: it brought to mind David Hume's preposterous attempts at courtship.

With imagination, no doubt, the director could have avoided the absurdity; but directors seem often more concerned these days with the conceptions in their minds than with the effects of their conceptions on the stage and on the audience.

There were other farcical elements in the production. Alfredo had, for some reason, brought a book to the party at the beginning of the opera, which he flung unmercifully about the stage (and picked up, so that he could fling it again).I am afraid that I was outraged at this treatment of a book, which was hardbound rather than a mere airport paperback, all the more so because he appeared subsequently to sing from its contents. And then, in another scene, he sat, singing passionately, on a great pile of books. I checked subsequently with members of the audience and they had all been distracted by the worry that the pile might collapse under Alfredo, making him look even more ridiculous than he already did as he sprawled among the volumes, an image that was so powerful in our minds that it was stronger than what we actually saw. It was made all the worse when Alfredo, standing up from the pile to our initial relief, having survived the ordeal, kicked the books and scattered them. Do poets kick books? I cannot say for certain that no poet ever kicked a book, but by scattering the books after he rose from sitting on them he made the audience wonder (again, I checked on this afterwards, that I was not alone in so wondering) whether there had been a mechanism by which the books were kept in a solid pile while he sat on them which then released them when it was time for them to be scattered by his kick. It is a very poor production that distracts an audience so.

No man is responsible for his own height, but the director was responsible for the titters that could be heard from the audience when Alfredo embraced his father, Germont. The man who sang Germont was about a foot taller than Alfredo, so that the son appeared to be embracing the father's waist or stomach, more like a little child than a grown man. Did the director not notice it, or was he living in some virtual world of his own abstract conception that, like a totalitarian dictator in charge of a country, he was determined to impose upon the little world that is a stage (all the stage's a world).

When Germont sings his famous aria requesting Violetta to forego the love of Alfredo for his daughter's sake, who will not be able to marry the man she loves if Alfredo continues to live with a woman of such ill-repute as Violetta, the daughter is actually made to appear on the stage, unceremoniously and unlovingly pushed to the fore by her father, dressed in a beret and grey gabardine mackintosh, and also wearing thick glasses. She looks about twelve, an awkward pubertal age, and more likely to grow up a bluestocking than a sensualist; even the most ferocious Moslems of ISIS would hardly have considered her old enough to marry. She was more Violet-Elizabeth in Just William, whose greatest utterance was *I'll thcream and thcream until I'm thick!*, than a future Cleopatra. Again the audience tittered, trying hard to suppress its mirth. What blindness struck the director that he could not see the effect the completely unnecessary appearance of this creature on the audience? It is characteristic of all the would-be or pseudo- great artists of our day that the effect on others of their work hardly concerns them.

The director also had the original, but not good, idea of introducing both Alfredo and his father into the auditorium. I haven't seen this done in an opera before, but it was reduced once more to absurdity as Alfredo struggled to get past the front row of the stalls like an embarrassed latecomer trying to gain his seat, on his way back on to the stage. A less romantic passage to anywhere could hardly be imagined and again the audience was reduced to subdued laughter. If bad production were a criminal offence, the German director, Peter Konwitschny, would be serving several life sentences for this production alone.

Of course there was an orgy scene, as there seems to be in so many opera productions these days, as if to justify our current propensity to exhibitionism by backdating it to an earlier epoch: for despite a setting in the modern world, no one could really believe that Traviata was truly contemporary, if for no other reason than that Violetta died of tuberculosis, as she would not have done today. Even the implicit protest that Traviata contains against the conventional social judgments of its day, its plea that love should be allowed to overcome or conquer social prejudice, is by now somewhat attenuated. In summary, this production of *Traviata* might more properly have been called *La Travestía* (not an Italian word, nor even Spanish, but a neologism appropriately neither English nor Italian).

I once saw a production of *Macbeth* in which the thane of Cawdor appeared on a balcony in pyjamas. At that point, I am afraid, I had to leave; there are some things too funny to be endured. But I didn't leave *Traviata*, and despite its abominations was able to enjoy it.

Now it so happened that I had told a friend of mine that I was going to see *Traviata*, and he was most disapproving. He was one of those art puritans who thinks that nothing but the very highest artistic achievement is worthy of our notice or enjoyment. Thus no painting is worth anything unless it be, say, Piero della Francesca or Velásquez (he had sneered at my fondness for Bronzino, for example, whom he regarded as vulgar). So it is with Verdi. In his opinion Joseph Green, as he insists on calling him as if he were the first to think of it, was little more than a turner-out of tunes for the hurdy-gurdy, fit to sell ice-creams by. He derisively hummed one of the melodies, or tunes as he would have called them, from the opera—which he calls *Triviata*.

In the first place, though, I do not agree that the only art that has a call on our attention is that of the very highest order. Our walls would be bare and our bookcases empty if we truly believed that. And it is partly, or even largely, by seeing or reading the inferior that we learn to recognise the superior. When the English critic, Cyril Connolly, wrote that *The more books we read, the clearer it becomes than the true function of a writer is to produce a masterpiece and that no other task is of any consequence,* he was guilty of mistaking rhetoric for good sense. The writer should always write as well as he is able, of course, but the term masterpiece is inherently a comparative one. In any case, a diet of masterpieces would leave us pretty constipated, and ignorant of many things into the bargain. And who would say that Edward Lear should not have written *The Owl and the Pussycat* merely because it did not aspire to be a Shakespeare sonnet?

Then, of course, there is the question of Verdi's status. I suspect that Verdi's immense popularity wherever western opera is performed, and that *Traviata* is probably the most frequently performed opera in the entire repertoire, affected his judgment. He is probably guilty of what might be called the snob's syllogism:

> What is popular is bad.
> *Traviata* is popular.
> Therefore *Traviata* is bad.

I would not go so far as to say that I have never myself been guilty of using a similar syllogism, and I cannot swear absolutely that I shall never do so again; it is probably rather less bad than the opposite:

> What is popular is good.
> *Traviata* is popular.
> Therefore *Traviata* is good.

But popularity of a century and a half is not quite the same as the popularity of the latest best-seller. Doctor Johnson was no admirer of the poet Thomas Gray, but he had this to say of the *Elegy*:

> In the character of his *Elegy* I rejoice to concur with the common reader; for by the common sense of readers uncorrupted with literary prejudices, after all the refinements of subtilty and the dogmatism of learning, must be finally decided all claim to poetical honours. The *Church-yard* abounds with images which find a mirrour in every mind, and with sentiments to which every bosom returns an echo.

May we not say something similar of *La Traviata*? It is not a knockdown argument, perhaps, but it as near to such as the subject in question can afford. But the director thought that he could go one better, as directors do these days.

33
Our Dreams Are Such Stuff As We Are Made On

THE OTHER NIGHT—actually, early in the morning—I had a strange and disturbing dream. Normally I do not attach much importance to the symbolism of my own dreams, which are often banal and indicative of a most elementary or basic need, such as that to relieve myself. But this dream was very odd; as usual, it woke me before its denouement, but unusually I was able to remember it, or a good part of it.

Two friends of mine had quarrelled and agreed to have a duel with revolvers. If the dream vouchsafed me the cause of their quarrel, I have forgotten it; but I do know that it was trivial and not worth losing a life over.

I was a second in this duel, which was appointed to take place a short time hence. During this time I asked a legal friend, a judge of one of the highest courts in the land, whether there was any legal step I could take to abort the duel. He assured me that there was not, but I did not really believe him even though he was incomparably more learned in the law than I. Surely in this day and age (an expression people use only in an argument of last resort) so primitive a manner of behaving had been outlawed?

The morning of the duel arrived. It was appointed for nine o'clock precisely. It was to take place in front of a medical school, though neither of the men who quarrelled was a doctor. The other second and I arrived on the duelling ground—a small patch of grass—at twenty to nine. For some reason this small detail was preserved in my memory. In the twenty minutes remaining, I was desperate to find a reason or means of stopping the duel.

I ran into the medical school because my lawyer had an office there (in my dream, that is). I was worried that he might not have arrived at work yet, but I knocked on his door marked Probyn and Co. (Probyn is the name of a character in a novel I had been reading the night before, and otherwise I knew no person of that name.) To my immense relief he was sitting at his desk. I recognised his face: it was that of my former literary agent, in the days when I still had one.

I was about to ask his advice when I suddenly thought of a solution myself: I would ask the police to come and arrest the duellers on a charge of conspiracy to murder, or illegal possession of firearms, and if necessary they could arrest us, the seconds, as accessories to these crimes—anything, but they must intervene.

This struck me in my dream as a brilliant, if obvious, solution, but I woke up before it could be put into operation. Perhaps the nightmare trauma of having to explain to the police on the telephone, and of convincing them that I was not just a time-waster or a crank, was more than my reticular activating system (the part of the brain that controls wakefulness and the transition between sleep and consciousness) could bear. I resolved to write down the dream before the memory of it faded, as it usually does.

One particular aspect of the dream puzzled me: not its illogicality or its implausibility, for we are all accustomed to the fact that dreams do not proceed as if they were a short story by Maupassant with a satisfyingly neat ending. It was rather that I felt a compulsion to continue to act as a second in the duel, that unless I could persuade the police to do as I asked I should have to go through with it, even unto the death of one of the duellers, and even though I knew the duel to be ridiculous. I could not just walk away from it.

Why not? It seemed a matter of honour, and the maintenance of honour was a stronger motive than any merely ethical consideration. But what is honour worth, asked Falstaff?

> Can honour set to a leg? no: or an arm? no: or take away the grief of a wound? no. Honour hath no skill in surgery, then? no. What is honour? a word. What is in that word honour? What is that honour? air. A trim reckoning! Who hath it? He that died o' Wednesday. Doth he feel it? No. Doth he hear it? no. 'Tis insensible, then. Yea,to the dead. But will it not live with the living? no. Why? detraction will not suffer it.

> Therefore I'll none of it. Honour is a mere scutcheon: and so ends my catechism.

This is the probably greatest indictment of honour as a virtue, or supposed virtue, in literature. In effect it reminds us not to run after false gods, so many of which are linked in some way to honour: titles, medals, prizes and so forth, which are all evanescent and ultimately ridiculous. Present mirth hath present laughter, to quote Feste the Fool (who was no fool); when you are dead, you are dead for a long time. Enjoy life while you have it and do not throw it away on an illusion.

But of course things are much more complex than Falstaff allows. If there is unease in our laughter at his speech because we know that in some circumstances he is right, when the standing on honour would be absurd and the throwing away of one's life foolhardy or reprehensible, we also know that he is prepared to use precisely the same argument to justify all dishonourable conduct whatsoever, in any circumstances. Like most of us, Falstaff is a philosopher after the fact; he uses philosophy to justify past actions, or actions that he has already decided upon, not to determine what action to take.

When I was asked, in some preliminary to my dream to which I do not have access, to be a second in the duel, I should have refused there and then; my initial acceptance was what started me on the downward slope to nightmare. I thought, or would have thought if I had thought of it at all, that to withdraw having first agreed would be a dishonourable thing to do. Therefore the descent was inexorable.

To break one's word is generally a dishonourable thing to do, and a world in which no one ever kept his word would be intolerable. Even in countries in which personal honesty is not the first characteristic, people must often be trusted in the small change of existence, usually with good result. But always to keep one's word, when circumstances have greatly changed, when to do so would cause useless hardship either to oneself or others, or when one should not have given one's word in the first place, turns honour into a species of spiritual pride. A man who says that he always keeps his word is either a liar or is to be avoided as pridefully inflexible.

Honour, then, is one of those virtues that is not free-standing, as it were. Whether or not it is a good thing depends on what the person is honourable about. You can admire the honour of an enemy or opponent up to certain point. He may, for example, refuse to take advantage of information that is discreditable to you, though not strictly relevant to the matter in hand, because it would be dishonourable to use it. To do so would be to infringe the rules of civilised opposition or debate to which he has agreed, implicitly or explicitly, beforehand: and he refuses such conduct even if it would secure him victory. The best recognition of his honour in so doing is not to resort to such conduct oneself, in other words to place a limit on what one is prepared to do oneself to secure victory.

But an enemy may be so dangerous or evil that even if he is honourable in some aspect of his conduct, the honour counts for nothing. If his cause is dreadful and he pursues it with vigour, then no conduct will extenuate it. Fidelity to others in joint pursuit of an atrocious end is not admirable but horrible and terrifying. In this respect, honour is like bravery: beyond a certain point of badness of cause, it is not, or should not be, the occasion of admiration.

Indeed, honour can turn into a kind of cowardice. Having agreed to act as a second in the duel, I dare not withdraw, as clearly I should have done. I did not want to go to my friend afterwards and tell him that, his duel being absurd and his willingness to kill his opponent abominable, I would have no further part in it. What was it that I feared?

A few moments' embarrassment, that's all. I did not want to face his reproach, his accusation of untrustworthiness. And to avoid this I was prepared to see him or his opponent go to his death. My honour was a device for disguising pusillanimity.

In public debate I try always to remain courteous (not with invariable success, but I try). Sometimes this courtesy slides into cowardice, however, my desire not to offend being greater than my attachment to truth, even when untruth (as I see it) is being propounded for someone I believe to be dishonest, unscrupulous or in some other way unworthy, an even when the untruth is a dangerous one. What is a virtue in many circumstances turns into a vice in others.

The fact that there is no precise point or moment at which virtue turns into vice suggests that there will never be any categorical imperatives, at least not of any use to the person who is trying to behave well. Kindness turns into cruelty when it helps to maintain the need for kindness to be exercised; it then becomes an exercise in self-congratulation rather than in doing good. On the other hand, laudable awareness of the need to avoid the point at which kindness transforms itself into cruelty or self-congratulation easily itself becomes indifference or callousness. The ethical life is a course steered eternally between Scylla and Charybdis, between the rock and the whirlpool of different manifestations of intransigence.

That there is no rule for discerning when virtue turns to vice does not mean that there is no real distinction between them, any more than the fact that there is no precise point at which a man becomes tall means there is no distinction between a tall man and a short one. No one has any difficulty in recognising the difference between an achondroplastic dwarf and an acromegalic giant. But the lack of such a rule is often used by people to justify conduct that has clearly passed over into vice, because the distinction between vice and virtue, having no decisive algorithm to distinguish them, is then (temporarily, for purposes of self-justification) held to be arbitrary and therefore unjust.

Did my dream mean anything? I have never dreamed of duels before, but oddly enough an antiquarian bookseller had sent me a catalogue some days before (printed catalogues, that so delight book-buyers, are going the way of books themselves) in which was offered for sale *A Hint on Duelling, in a Letter to a Friend*, published in 1751, and of which only two other copies are known.

The bookseller has evidently read the book and writes:

> The author [unknown] would not have duelling entirely suppressed, but suggests the establishment of a proper Court of Honour would lessen the frequency of the practice…

and he then quotes the author:

> The Decision of Men of adequate Character and Authority would in most Cases after Insults received prevent Duels; and where that fail'd, a due-proportioned Punishment judiciously and impartially inflicted would soon lessen the Frequency of the Practice.

And the friend to whom I was to be second in the duel had recently invited me to give a talk at a conference in Illyria, and I been recently engaged on writing an essay on the character of Malvolio (*Twelfth Night*, you will vaguely remember, takes place in Illyria).

Our dreams, then, are such stuff as we are made on. Could it really be otherwise, and does it matter? I doubt it.

34
Cuckoo about Cuckoos

WHEN I WAS A BOY I used to collect wild birds' eggs, but I think I always knew that I had no serious purpose in doing so and that the passion would not last. I had not the patience of a real ornithologist; rather I was beguiled by the joys of the chase, the beauty of the eggs and pleasures of possession. Luckily I never took the eggs of any but the commonest birds, so that my contribution to the decline of bird populations was very minor. I suppose that for every hundred boys who go bird-nesting, only one becomes a true nature-lover.

I wish now that I had taken a more serious interest in the natural world when I was young (along with many other things). I suppose this amounts almost to wishing that I had been a different person, which is absurd; but yet the wish returned to me very strongly as I read recently a most wonderful book about cuckoos, called *Cuckoo*, by the professor of behavioural ecology at Cambridge, Nick Davies.

Here I must confess to a prejudice against authors, especially very learned ones, who call themselves by diminutives of their first names, but it took only a page or two of this book for me to overcome it in this case. I read the book at a sitting, though it was nearly three hundred pages long. I have seldom read a book about nature with such unalloyed pleasure.

Part of the pleasure, perhaps, was an awareness that I was reading completely without ulterior motive, for the sheer interest of the thing, as I seldom have the opportunity of doing: dull would he be of soul who saw no fascination in the conduct of these extraordinary birds. As the author points out, the nightingale has a more beautiful song, but the cuckoo has more metaphors.

Professor Davies is the man I wish I could have been. He has studied cuckoos and performed conceptually simple but practically difficult experiments on them in the same area of fenland ten miles out of Cambridge, for more than thirty years, that is to say for half his earthly existence. I do not mean that he is a monomaniac or a man whose intelligence is a narrow beam rather than a broad one, far from it: rather he is the kind of man who is able:

> To see a World in a Grain of Sand
> And a Heaven in a Wild Flower,
> Hold Infinity in the palm of your hand
> And Eternity in an hour.

His love of nature is evident in all he writes; he is a keen admirer of Darwin (as anyone who reads him must be), and his study of cuckoos provides convincing evidence of, or at least arguments for, Darwinian evolution that is taking place at a considerably faster rate than we usually suppose. If Professor Davies has no religious belief, he is certainly a nature mystic—as indeed was Darwin—believing that the world we have inherited is full of beauty and fascination, if we would but look at it with attention.

We infuse the world with meaning because it is impossible for us as humans not to do so. A purely mechanical view of the world is thus impossible for us. We may be evolved creatures, the product of natural selection, descended from the virus or the bacterium, but we have reached a stage at which moral and aesthetic judgment cannot be eliminated from our thought or consciousness: and, since goodness and beauty are not qualities that can be found measured in Angstrom units or light years, the attempt to reduce Man to a mere physical being is destined to fail, at least in the sense that no one could live as if it were true.

Indeed, there is evidence of this impossibility in the words of Darwin himself that Professor Davies quotes in the course of his book, including the famous last words of The Origin of Species:

> There is a grandeur in this view of life… from so simple a beginning endless forms most beautiful and most wonderful have been, and are being evolved.

Or again:

> When I view all beings not as special creations, but as the lineal descendants of some few beings which lived long before the first of the Cambrian system was deposited, they seem to me to become ennobled.

Beautiful, wonderful, ennobled: these are not the terms of naturalism, and in my view cannot be translated successfully into the language of naturalism. Of course, Darwin didn't have to use them at all: his book would have been none the less compelling, scientifically, if he had not. But it seems to me extremely unlikely that Darwin would ever have undertaken his profound studies of animate nature without having first been convinced that it was beautiful, wonderful, and important, a word he used in a letter to the great naturalist Bateson, who first described mimicry, to describe his, Bateson's, first scientific paper. Importance is a moral quality, for something can be important only according to a scale of values; no amount of looking down a microscope or through a telescope will reveal importance, and it is as useless to expect it as it would be to use a rubber stamp to boil potatoes.

It is curious that even the most convinced evolutionists find it difficult to eviscerate their language of intention, design and moral assessment. They claim that this language is a kind of shorthand, and that it would be tedious to translate such language into a purely naturalistic one: but I suspect that this is not really quite honest, and that in fact they not only speak, but think in this shorthand. At any rate, they conceive of Evolution as if it had designs as an entity rather than an abstraction—Evolution does this, Evolution does that—when, of course, the whole point of the concept is to explain how we became what we are without resort to design, Evolution's or anything or anybody else's. And I say this as one who does not believe in any overall purpose immanent in the universe, though I concede that I cannot prove it one way or the other.

It is particularly difficult to refrain from investing cuckoos with non-natural qualities. Their behaviour seems to us outrageous, even criminal. Never mind that they have tiny brains, are presumably incapable of moral distinctions and act out of instinct. When the cuckoo chick throws the eggs of the legitimate owners out of the nest, or even worse heaves the legitimate chicks out, we feel a sense of outrage. But the cuckoo can do what Luther said that he could do: in other words, no other. When Professor Davies told passers-by that he was searching for cuckoo eggs, they assumed that he would destroy them, as being those of a vicious and parasitical creature, rather than conduct scientific experiments to discover why it was that birds parasitized by cuckoos did not recognise cuckoos' eggs and persisted in feeding cuckoo chicks though they had actually witnessed these chicks destroying their own offspring. And, indeed, it is astonishing to see photographs of small birds feeding chicks grown to eight times their own size: we would think it absurd if we were not mildly appalled. It offends our sense of justice and decency.

Indeed, Professor Davies himself cannot refrain using words of moral evaluation when he describes the behaviour of other birds that use cuckoo-like chick-rearing techniques. He says of a bird called the honeyguide, for example, that its conduct is 'as chilling as any horror story.' Honeyguides are so-called because, in Africa, they guide humans to bees' nests, and are therefore very liked and well-respected. 'However,' writes Professor Davies, 'there is a darker side to their apparently sweet nature.' And that dark side is that the female lays its egg in the nest of bee-eaters, which are in a tunnel underground:

> The honeyguide [chick] grabs a host chick using its bill tip, then repeatedly bites and shakes its victim for up to four minutes at a time. The bites rarely cause open wounds, but lead to haemorrhaging under the skin and heavy bruising... From the time of the first attack, they take from nine minutes to over seven hours to die.

Because of the darkness, the bee-eaters do not see what is going on, 'the horror' as Professor Davies calls it, and feed the honeyguide chick even as it is killing the bee-eater chicks (I confess that here I thought of foreign Muslim clerical fanatics in England receiving social security payments even as they call for the destruction of the society that pays them). We are horrified, it is true; but all the participants in the scene are acting only according to their nature. Our horror is a sign that we have transcended nature.

No tribute of mine can do justice, though, to the fascination of Professor Davies' researches (and those of others in the field). For example, he discovered why it was that host birds continue to feed the single cuckoo chick as much as they would have fed their four legitimate chicks had they survived. The cuckoo chick makes urgent begging sounds at a much higher rate than the 'real' chicks would have done; and it is these sounds which stimulate its step-parents to respond by finding food with which to feed it.

I had always thought of the cuckoo as an English bird: after all, the earliest known poem in English begins:

> Sumer is icumen in,
> Lhude sing cuccu...

but, of course, it spends only a small portion of its life in England—three months at most—and it spends most of its life in the process of migration. Oddly enough, it never occurred to me to wonder where the cuckoo spent the rest of his life. But with astonishing ingenuity, by means of satellite tracking, its pattern of migration has been traced. The cuckoo (at least the male of the species) flies from England down across Europe and North Africa, stopping on the way to feed, and either flies via West Africa or across the Sahara to the Congo, where is stays for about three months, before returning north, not necessarily by the same route as it travelled south. The cuckoo is thus as much a Congolese bird as an English one, it all depends on your perspective.

The population of cuckoos has declined by 65 per cent in Britain since 1980. I cannot claim that cuckoos have played a big part in my life before reading this book, but nevertheless I should be deeply, perhaps even disproportionately, saddened if I knew that at some time in the near future this harbinger of spring and summer would never be heard again.

Why has there been this precipitous decline in numbers? It is far greater than the decline in the numbers of the birds in whose nests cuckoos lay their eggs. The answer appears to be that, to breed successfully, cuckoos need to time their egg-laying precisely, so that their chicks hatch in time successfully to destroy their competitors in the nests. But while cuckoos migrate according to the length of days, the birds whom they parasitise nest and lay according to temperature, and since spring comes earlier now than it did (thanks to global warming), the cuckoos arrive too late to optimise their egg-laying. Of course, some other explanation may emerge.

Professor Davies provides many startling examples in his wonderful book, which I urge everyone to read, of natural selection in action. All the same, I had the nagging feeling, of which I could not quite disembarrass myself however hard I tried, that the argument from natural selection was more logically circular than strictly empirical, and that such was the ingenuity of the human mind that it could easily find an explanation for any trait or characteristic of any creature that was compatible with natural selection. Directly opposite traits were equally explicable by it; and it is probably logically, not empirically, impossible that surviving creatures should have survived because they were selected for survival. The theory is saved from banality by differentials in survival between naturally occurring variations (and also during changes in naturally-occurring or Man-induced circumstances). Professor Davies explains beautifully why some characteristics, for example egg-markings, that are advantageous in one set of conditions, will be lost when those circumstances change so that they become disadvantageous to survival, and give examples in his magisterial book.

But why do we find a beautiful explanation beautiful?

35
There Are No Flies On Us

GOOD WILL is necessary but not sufficient: a painful lesson in life and one that has often to be relearned because it is so easily and wilfully forgotten. Benevolence can often be useless or even on some occasions harmful and our best intentions may be misunderstood and taken for the opposite.

A pair of flycatchers nested this year in the eaves of our house in France. It was pleasant and amusing to sit on the terrace in the evening and watch the parent birds fly back and forth to feed the nestlings, having caught insects on the wing with their darting flight. The nestlings chirruped loudly for food as the mother or father bird approached, and for some reason we laughed at the sound.

Then one day a nestling fell out of the nest on to the terrace below. Although there are cuckoos around, I think it was an accident; the other nestlings continued their chirrups, and a cuckoo would have ejected them all, not just one.

The fallen nestling was quite far advanced in its development. It was covered in feathers not down, and its tail feathers were a russet brown in distinction to the rest of its body, whose feathers were grey-brown.. It could almost fly but not quite: when we approached it hopped away and seemed when it did so to keep itself suspended in the air by flapping its wings a little longer than just a hop would have enabled to do. It was like watching an avian re-enactment of the Wright Brothers' first experiments.

We at once became fond of the little bird and anxious for its future. It was an appealing creature with bright little eyes and a solemn expression. All those insects brought by mother and father bird had made him (or her) quite rotund.

We are not ornithologists, my wife and I, and therefore not well-versed in the habits of flycatchers. Sometimes the little bird would hop into the house and perch on the bottom bar of a chair, chirping not cheerfully, as it had sounded in the nest, but with something between melancholy and desperation. It wanted, presumably, to draw its parents' attention to its plight, to let them know its whereabouts so that they could continue to feed it. (Can a bird truly be said to 'want' anything?) If it was not fed, presumably it would die quite quickly.

When we approached it, it hopped back out on to the terrace, where there was a greater chance that its parents would see and hear it. But we had no confidence in bird brains: birds perform seeming miracles such as migration across half the world, but unthinkingly, inflexibly, because, like Luther at Wittenberg, they can do no other. Faced by a new situation, such as a fallen fledgling, they are not very adaptable—or so we imagined.

We knew, of course, that Nature is red in tooth and claw and that fledglings die by the thousand or the million every season. They fall out of nests and are crushed; they are predated by snakes and rats and weasels, and even by other birds of their own species, and that therefore our fledgling flycatcher was of no special significance in the larger scheme of things. But we all live in small rather than large schemes. The abstract knowledge was entirely vitiated by the plight of this one bird, whom we at once invested with personality and suffering. As Stalin said, admittedly in another context, one death is a tragedy, a million is a statistic.

There was nothing we could do, however, to persuade it of our good intention. As in politics, so in Nature: there are no friends, only interests. Natural selection had programmed the little creature to regard all others as predators and all out cooing and reassuring words failed to change its attitude towards us. I suppose that if we were approached by a creature several hundred times our size we too would not be much reassured by its expressions of goodwill towards us, even if we could understand them.

We wanted to feed the bird so that it should not die: but on what? We thought that it was not very far from independence, so our attentions would be necessary only for a day or two, a few days at most. My wife thought we might put a shallow bowl of water or of milk before it, but I said that I thought birds did not drink, certainly not milk: milk, after all, is mammalian. She also tried scattering some muesli before it, in the hope that it might be tempted to peck at it, but I said that I did not think that flycatchers ate muesli, not even the organic variety, as this was, left behind by some guests last year who were more concerned for the state of their bowels than the aesthetics of their breakfast and feared that we did not have a rigorous attitude ourselves to the healthiness of our diet.

Do flycatchers eat muesli? The answer appeared to be no, as I always thought it would be. Flycatchers eat flies, they don't catch flies for the sheer fun or pleasure of it. So my wife began to gather some insects, with which our house and garden are plentifully supplied. The problem is sometimes not so much to catch them as to avoid them: if you are not careful, they get in the fruit and the sauce and the wine. We feel none of the tenderness for them that we felt for the fledgling, except perhaps for the type of large beetle that somehow gets on to its back and cannot right itself: those we give a helping hand.

There are more varieties of insect, however, than of any other kind of multicellular creature (the insects, though not necessarily meek or humble, shall inherit the earth). The insects that we caught for our fledgling did not tempt it, and its beak remained resolutely shut when we held one before it, or even put one on the ground before it. You can lead a bird to a bug, but you can't make it eat. We realised that, because of our ignorance, we should have to let Nature, red or not in tooth and claw, take its course.

In fact, the parents birds seemed to take an interest in their fallen fledgling. Whether they actually fed him we could not see, because as soon as they noticed our presence they flew off, but they landed near it as they had not landed before. Perhaps the whole situation had been a normal one (for flycatchers), and not an incipient tragedy as we had assumed. Perhaps the story will end happily, with the fledgling reaching maturity thanks to continued feeding by its parents (assuming that an adult flycatcher's life is a happy one). We do not like to think of the alternative: the picture of the sweet, solemn little bird is before our eyes. At least there are no cats locally to have preyed on it.

The story illustrates how quickly and easily we may become sentimental, and how that sentimentality may lead to incontinent benevolence. I remember reading somewhere that seemingly orphaned fledglings should be left alone at least for several hours until it is established beyond doubt that they have been abandoned to their fate, for trying to help them can actually harm them and cause the very abandonment that such help is intended to rectify. But fools—ignorant, benevolent fools—rush in where angels—knowledgeable, experienced angels—fear to tread.

There are many areas of life in which this lesson is important, particularly medicine, politics, controversy and private life. The desire to help, however genuine or burning, is not the same as actually helping. Doctors, for example, grow more sceptical of their own powers as they grow older, surgeons less aggressively interventionist, all of them more aware of the harms that they inadvertently cause than they were at the beginning of their careers, when they assumed that to do something was always better than to do nothing, and that any harms were worth the price they made the patients pay. The history of medicine is full of terrible things done by doctors to patients, all with the best of intentions: serious operations for conditions or causes of conditions that did not exist, such as floating kidney or dental sepsis as the origin of psychosis. The list is long: I once reviewed a history of medicine that related that history only through the terrible sufferings doctors had put their patients through in the name of cure. Our knowledge is better-founded now than ever before, but still if you read the medical journals you find whole categories of patients treated rigorously with unpleasant drugs or risky procedures to no benefit to themselves. In other words, the urge to help should be kept under rational control, like any other urge, though not so completely that it withers all sympathy with suffering or all impulse to go to the assistance of anybody whatever his circumstances.

In politics, it hardly needs emphasis, good intentions are not enough, though naturally enough politicians always claim them and resort to them as a defence when their policies are universally accepted as having been disastrous. Credit for success, absolution for failure, that is what politicians (being human, or almost human) seek. No one acknowledges being of the Devil's party (except a few Satanists, whose concept of evil is usually very limited and even childish, confined to boiling lizards alive in darkened rooms while they, the Satanists, cast their malign but ineffectual spells and stick pins into effigies of people whom they do not like).

In controversy there is always the temptation to take the nicer side, for those who are right often seem hard and unfeeling. But to be nice is not automatically to be right, even if it were not also the case that good intentions often disguise a substratum of malice: sympathy is sometimes a veneer of sadism. As La Rochefoucauld said, there is in the misfortunes of our friends something not entirely displeasing: the truth of which one acknowledges as soon as it is one reads it, though with a feeling of guilt. That is why doing good by causing others to suffer is pleasurable, and why malevolence in politics is always so much stronger than benevolence.

In private matters, virtues such as honesty are likewise often but a veneer for sadism, for example in telling the truth about or to someone. The tone of self-righteousness is often discernible in malicious gossip, or should I say the tone of malice in self-righteous gossip? At any rate, we enjoy enumerating the defects of others, and not for their own good either.

This is not to say that complete and sincere benevolence does not or cannot exist. Our feelings towards the fledgling flycatcher were purely benevolent, even if later in the day we dined off guinea fowl and could therefore be accused of inconsistency or hypocrisy. True benevolence is true benevolence even if it does not spread itself to the entire class of cases to which it ought to spread itself if it were to be entirely consistent. That kind of benevolence, I think, is beyond human powers, though intellectuals claim that the inevitable hypocrisy of benevolence consequent upon this impossibility more than cancels out its virtue. An intellectual is a person who prefers abstract consistency to common decency, at least in his pronouncements. (In actual life, though, he may espouse the most horrible abstract principle but act with common decency.)

There is, or should be, a constant interplay between good will and intellectual activity. It should not be a question of the good rushing in where the cynical refuse to act. Perhaps if my wife and I had known more about flycatchers, and what to do in such situations, we could have saved the fledgling's life—assuming, that is, that it was lost, an assumption that is likewise beyond our knowledge. Good intentions can no more redeem abysmal ignorance than can encyclopaedic knowledge redeem an ill will.

36
Of Tyrants and Trillions, Part I

TYRANNY IS QUITE WRONG, of course, on that we are all agreed, but neither can anyone deny that tyrants fascinate us. Indeed, where would Latin American literature have been without them? The most famous book of only the second Latin American author to win the Nobel Prize, Miguel Ángel Asturias, was *El Señor Presidente*, a denunciation in fiction of the Guatemalan dictator Cabrera. Gabriel García Márquez, another winner of the Nobel Prize, wrote *The Autumn of the Patriarch*, whose protagonist exhibited features of both Rojas Pinilla of Colombia and Goméz of Venezuela. A third winner of the Nobel Prize, Mario Vargas Llosa, wrote a novel, *La fiesta del chivo*, about the assassinated dictator of the Dominican Republic, Trujillo. And by far the most famous book by the eminent Paraguayan writer, Roa Bastos, was *Yo, el Supremo*, about the early nineteenth century Paraguayan dictator, Dr José Gaspar Rodríguez de Francia, who remains perhaps the most interesting of the many interesting Latin American despots, for whom Thomas Carlyle was something of an apologist. Many are the stories told of Latin American dictators, no doubt some of them apocryphal but all of them nonetheless believable, which no doubt says something about the region's political culture. Two of my favourites concern Justo Rufino Barrios of Guatemala, who was once allegedly seen to take a copy of the Guatemalan constitution, fold it in four, put it on a chair and sit on it, and General Mariano Melgarejo of Bolivia, who said 'I am going to rule in Bolivia as long as I like, and I'll hang anyone who disagrees from the nearest tree.' He was also reputed to have marched his troops over the balcony of the presidential palace to demonstrate their loyalty to him to a visiting dignitary. When Prussia invaded France in 1870, he wanted to send the Bolivian army to help France, dispatching it (as he thought) overland across the Atlantic. As this suggests, good anecdotes do not necessarily mean good governance.

If revenge is a dish best eaten cold, tyranny is a phenomenon best enjoyed from a distance. The other day I was walking in a district of London best known for its low pleasures and its second-hand bookshops (the former in the ascent and the latter in decline) when I passed a shop that specialised in the sale of banknotes: not foreign exchange, but banknotes as objects of interest in themselves.

I have always liked banknotes, finding them both fascinating and (often) beautiful. In the window of the shop was a little collection, not very expensive, called The Tyrant Collection. The tyrants portrayed on banknotes were—in no particular order of ferocity—Idi Amin of Uganda, Mao of China, Saddam Hussein of Iraq, the Ayatollah Khomeini of Iran, Kim Il Sung of North Korea, and Separmurat Niyazov of Turkmenistan. I couldn't resist: I entered the shop.

Of course, there are serious and learned collectors of banknotes, just as there are serious and learned bibliophiles, numismatists and philatelists, and no doubt the owners of the shop preferred to deal with serious customers rather than with ignorant casual ones such as I: for no one could run such a shop without being impassioned by its stock-in-trade, or by being motivated only by the desire to make money (no pun intended). Rather sheepishly, therefore, I asked for the Tyrant Collection, fearing to reveal thereby the frivolity of my custom.

The gentleman at the counter turned to a woman behind him (I forget her name, but will make up one for her) and said, 'Jane, pass me a Tyrant.' There were little packs of these banknotes already made up, and she duly passed him a Tyrant.

'Anything else?' he asked.

There was: I had seen in the window also the last banknote struck before the downfall of Colonel Gaddafi, of a rather handsome blue design, with the smiling colonel himself with what appears like a very large bath towel wrapped around his head (the colonel made up his folkloric costumes as he went along). It was slightly more expensive, but I thought it would go very well with the Tyrant which, oddly enough, was somewhat lacking in blue as a colour.

After I left the shop, the words 'Pass me a Tyrant' remained in my mind. Somehow they seemed to me a concise and elegant way of expressing the absurdity and transience of power and its pretensions. The characters portrayed on the banknotes once made millions tremble at their command, and even the mere utterance of their name must have caused millions of hearts skip a beat in fear: and yet, only a relatively short time after their deaths, these self-appointed deciders of millions of destinies were mockingly consigned to a collective appellation. I thought of Shelley's great poem on this theme:

> I met a traveller from an antique land
> Who said: "Two vast and trunkless legs of stone
> Stand in the desert. Near them, on the sand,
> Half sunk, a shattered visage lies, whose frown,
> And wrinkled lip, and sneer of cold command,
> Tell that its sculptor well those passions read
> Which yet survive, stamped on these lifeless things,
> The hand that mocked them and the heart that fed:
> And on the pedestal these words appear:
> 'My name is Ozymandias, king of kings:
> Look on my works, ye Mighty, and despair!'
> Nothing beside remains. Round the decay
> Of that colossal wreck, boundless and bare
> The lone and level sands stretch far away.

One should always remember, I suppose, that this Olympian detachment, this ironic view of the matter, is not possible for those unfortunate enough to have lived through tyrannies of the thoroughness of Niyazof or Kim Il Sung; and also that it is not only the pretensions of tyranny that will suffer the fate of Ozymandias, but all the things that we non-tyrants think are important.

Be that as it may, I was happy with my tyrants and bore them triumphantly home. Then I had the happy idea of having them framed, one on top of the other in gradually increasing size, and took them the following day to the local framer. He was delighted with them too, in fact he cooed with delight. Mostly he has to frame banal wedding photographs or the like, and so an original commission pleased him enormously. In fact he was so taken with my tyrants that he asked me whether, when next I was in London, I could buy him some as a present for his brother, a man who had everything (except for Tyrants). I said that I would.

We spent a few happy moments, the framer and I, choosing the right mount and frame for the tyrants, and a few days later I received a text message: 'Tyrants ready for collection.' When I returned to his shop, he was still smiling irrepressibly. I must say that the tyrants looked extremely fine in their frame with a black mount and a slender gilt lining to the frame: a gradient from the smallest of the notes at the top to the largest at the bottom, all most tastefully shaded as to colour. The framer was proud of his handiwork, as well he might be.

At the top was Mao, dressed in his pseudo-proletarian jacket expressly designed to give the impression of humility and equality with the humblest of his fellow countrymen, though he was in fact as unbridled in the satisfaction of his appetites as any divine-right monarch of Louis XIV's time: and, of course, with infinitely less refinement and taste. It is given to modern tyrannies to build sometimes on a gigantic scale but to leave nothing behind of any aesthetic value, things worthy only of demolition.

Below Mao comes Idi Amin, all in a kind of faeculent brown. He wears the uniform of a British senior officer, a general at least (he pronounced himself a Field Marshal). His entirely British uniform is symbolic of his ambivalent relationship to the formerly colonising power and its culture. On the one hand he was humiliated by the subordinate and even lowly status it accorded him and would have continued to accord him had the colonial regime remained. On the other hand, he admired it and wished to emulate it. He resolved this contradiction by dressing himself up in a uniform that conferred on him one of the highest ranks within its hierarchy, revenging himself on it and taking part in it at the same time.

Then comes Gaddafi, as mentioned already with his strange bath-towel turban. His pose is that of a thinker: the back of one hand supports the elbow of his other arm as he caresses the left side of his face with the palm of the hand, while gazing smilingly but shrewdly. He always wanted to be known as a thinker, of course and hoped that his own book, *The Green Book*, would rival Mao's *Little Red Book* in influence. His search, or perhaps thirst would be a better word, for originality led him to dress in bizarre ways never seen before or since, and unique to himself. His desire for originality, however, was in itself a manifestation of the influence of romantic individualism that reached even the backwater of Tripoli.

Below Gaddafi comes Niyazov, whose inner klepto- and megalomaniac was released by the collapse of the Soviet Union. Until then a faithful, dutiful and successful communist, he decided that the future belonged to nationalism. A dictator's dictator, he decreed after his heart surgery not only that he, but everyone else, should give up smoking, and banned smoking in public places: a policy for which the British Medical Association, spiritual heir to Niyazov, is now actively lobbying.

Then comes the Ayatollah. His banknote is one of the two that does not have a single letter or figure in the Latin alphabet or western numeration, the other being that of his sworn enemy, Saddam Hussein. The portrait of the Ayatollah, a good one, shows him peering to his right, his expression not that of a spiritual leaders but of a shrewd, worldly and ruthless man of politics. There is not much in the way of compromise, forgiveness or kindness in that face, never mind spirituality: it is the face of a man who, if he worshipped anything, worshipped himself.

Below him is the only one of the tyrants on whom I personally ever clapped eyes: Kim Il Sung. On this banknote he appears in the Stalino-Mao costume that he then favoured, rather than the light grey western suit with grey shoes (no gentleman wears grey shoes) that he favoured when I saw him. Oddly enough, the Albanian leader, Enver Hoxha, favoured suits of the same cloth as Kim Il Sung's, and it is a fair bet that they were the only people in their respective countries permitted to wear a suit made of it. The roundel in which Kim Il Sung stares full-face on from the banknote is surrounded by flowers, probably the variety known in North Korea as the Kimilsungia. In North Korea they managed to make even flowers sinister.

Last but not least comes Saddam Hussein. In the background is a mediaeval battle, presumably with Saladin in the lead. The latter, of course, was a Kurd, a nation whom Saddam had a tendency to gas; but one of the first victims of tyranny is irony. That is not to say that no one regrets the demise of the Saddam regime: the Christians of Iraq, for example. It is a tribute to the infinite ingenuity of Man that the downfall of a monstrous government can result in a worse life for quite large numbers of people.

Saddam has something in common with Idi Amin: the uniform that he wears is of purely British design, down to the general's flashes on the collar. Who would not be proud of so deep a legacy in so disparate a pair of countries as Iraq and Uganda (both creations of the British, incidentally)? Every time I look on my collection of tyrants, my heart will swell with patriotic pride.

I should have mentioned that, while buying my tyrants, I also bought a Zimbawean banknote of fifty trillion Zimbabwean dollars: that is to say 50,000,000,000,000. I have a small collection too of hyperinflation banknotes, of which more another time.

37
Of Tyrants and Trillions, Part II

HAVING FRAMED my Tyrant collection, together with Colonel Gaddafi, I rummaged around among the banknotes that I had brought home from my travels to various parts of the world, and realised that I had yet more tyrants to frame. Mostly, though not entirely, they were African. I also had an incipient hyperinflation collection, though in some cases the two categories overlapped.

For example banknotes from the Mobutu era in Zaire (now once more the Congo) belonged to both categories, tyrant and hyperinflation: in the end, I opted to include Mobutu in the tyrants. Lenin likewise, though he was one of the few tyrants who ever really understood the terribly destructive effects of inflation—which, however, he welcomed because economic cataclysm was the midwife of communist revolution. In 1919, while Lenin was still at the helm of Russian affairs, Keynes began in his essay on inflation:

> Lenin is said to have declared that the best way to destroy the Capitalist system was to debauch the currency... As the inflation proceeds and the real value of the currency fluctuates from month to month, all permanent relations between debtors and creditors, which form the ultimate foundation of capitalism, become so utterly disordered as to be almost meaningless; and the process of wealth-getting degenerates into a gamble and a lottery.
>
> Lenin was certainly right. There is no subtler, no surer means of overturning the existing basis of Society than to debauch

> the currency... If prices are continually rising, every trader who has purchased for stock or owns property and plant inevitably makes profits. By directing hatred against this class, therefore, the... governments are carrying a step further the fatal process which the subtle mind of Lenin had consciously conceived.

And in vain do you try to persuade most people that hoarding in times of inflation is a symptom of inflation, not its cause. That is because we find it easier (and more gratifying) to blame the supposed villains who are close to hand.

A German friend of mine who lives in England told me that his grandfather had invested all his savings in mortgages and that when the great inflation came they were all redeemed in exchange for a piece of paper so valueless that robbers would throw whole stashes of them away in order to take the case in which they were being carried. You were robbed for your wallet, not for what it contained. I have a 1000 mark banknote of the period—rather handsome, with a prosperous fifteenth-century burgher of the Fugger type on it—heavily overprinted by *One Milliard Marks* (1,000,000,000). No doubt a folk memory of this is part of the reason the Germans are so attached to a currency that maintains its value, or loses it only slowly.

To avoid the anger that creditors expropriated in this way understandably felt in Germany, I believe the Brazilians, during one of their periods of hyperinflation, re-valued mortgages *pari passu* with inflation so that mortgagees could not take advantage of it in this way, to pay off debts contracted in good, or at least better, money with bad.

In framing my new tryant and hyperinflation collections, I had to decide on who was a tyrant and what constituted hyperinflation. There was no doubt that Macías Nguema of Equatorial Guinea, self-designated as *El Único Milagro*, the Only Miracle, was a tyrant; if a man who regarded the possession of printed matter as in itself suspicious of treason, reduced output of the principal export crop by 90 per cent despite (or was it because of?) near universal forced labour, and either killed or drove into exile a third of the population, was not a tyrant, who was? The green 100 *Ekwele* note, with its portrait of the Unique Miracle, printed in London by Thomas de la Rue and Company, is very handsome, however.

But what of Julius Nyerere, *Mwalimu* (Teacher), of Tanzania? Was he a tyrant? He didn't much care for opposition, kept a large number of political prisoners, and 'villagised' 70 per cent of the population—that is to say, drove peasants into semi-collectivised villages—with predictable effects on agricultural production. And yet he did not have the stigmata of a *full-blown* African tyrant. Despite his adoption of Mao-type costume after a state visit to China, during which huge crowds turned out to greet him (until then, he had worn a collar and tie or safari suit like a normal chap), and which he assumed was a spontaneous outburst of enthusiasm for his person, he was not truly bizarre. He even had his good points, as I now see in retrospect: he was genuinely no tribalist, and as for corruption, he kept it within limits. I have a book by him inscribed to an old friend of his, a British fellow-traveller of his villageisation scheme, and he had very refined handwriting, that of an educated and cultivated man (he translated some of Shakespeare into Swahili). So in the end I decided he was not really bad enough to qualify as one of my tyrants.

As in most things in life, however, it was hard to be entirely consistent. I decided to include El Haj Omar (formerly Jean-Bernard) Bongo of Gabon among the tyrants, though he was not really the worst. But what *le Grand Camarade* (the Great Comrade) lacked in stature—he always wore platform shoes in public and no one in any photograph published in his country was allowed to appear taller than he, much as churches in Moslem countries are not allowed to be higher than mosques—he made up for in longevity as dictator.

About General Momoh of Sierra Leone I had few doubts. When I look at him I think of what the American ambassador to Paraguay, Mr Washburn, said of the second head of state of that country, Carlos Antonio López: he so loved his country that he owned half of it. Momoh, by contrast, looked as though he so loved his country that he had *eaten* half of it. He looks out at one with a kind of greasy, post-prandial satisfaction.

I decided to include Jean-Claude Duvalier among my new tyrants for two reasons: banknotes bearing his portrait appear to be rare, and I have a sentimental attachment to Haiti. Whether a man so weak, foolish and easily manipulated as he really deserved to be called a tyrant (when really he was a figurehead)—unlike his father, Papa Doc, who was undoubtedly a real tyrant—is perhaps doubtful.

Interestingly, two of the worst tyrants of the twentieth century, Hitler and Stalin, never appeared on banknotes of their own countries. What, if anything, this means I do not know.

There were definitional problems too with hyperinflation. When does 'ordinary' inflation (such as most mortgagees have benefited from, at least if they have not been foolish) become the *hyper* variety. (I suppose it is the same problem with children: when does their activity become *hyper*? When the patience of adults run out, I suppose.)

In the end, I decided on a crude measure: once a currency had a banknote of the 100,000 denomination, there must have been hyperinflation. By the standards of some banknotes produced, 100,000 may not seem very much, but appearances can be misleading. The case of Peru is instructive. In my hyperinflation collection, for example, is a banknote for a paltry-seeming 100,000 *Intis*; but it must be remembered that the new *Inti* had already replaced the old *Sol*, at a rate of one to a million, so that 100,000 Intis was 1,000,000,000,000 old *Soles*.

I was in Peru with a friend at the time of the hyperinflation. Not surprisingly, you couldn't buy much with *Intis*: for anything worth more than a few trillion, you had to pay in dollars. For small purchases, however, it was best to pay in *Intis*. You conserved your dollars for big purchases, such a paperback book. Lining the main roads were money-changers, waving huge wads of paper currency to entice you to change.

My friend and I decided one afternoon to have a cup of tea. Has we enough *Intis* with us? We thought of changing some money at 90,000 *Intis* to the dollar, *i.e.* 90,000,000,000 *Soles*, but decided against: we probably had sufficient for now. On our way back about 20 minutes later, the dollar was at 110,000 *Intis*, or 110,000,000,000 *Soles*. It was two or three decades later before we became accustomed to figures such as these, and then it was for entire national debts rather than for the price of a cup of tea. As Paul Krugman would no doubt say, this shows that there is still plenty of scope for quantitative easing.

One of my favourite hyperinflation banknotes, aesthetically-speaking, is a Turkish one, for the comparatively modest figure of ten million Turkish *Lira*. From this splendid blue and red creation stares the face of Kemal Ataturk. I am an admirer of Ataturk's, though now that we have reached a stage of complete enlightenment we cannot possibly agree with all his policies. Ataturk stares at us head on, in his western garb of stiff collar, cravat and black cutaway coat. I mean no disrespect to Ataturk (still, I believe, a crime in Turkey, Erdogan notwithstanding) when I say that on this banknote he looks like a stage hypnotist, with his penetrating gaze that seems to goes straight to your weak spot. When you come to think of it, this is perhaps the whole secret of leadership, that is to say penetration to your followers' weak spots. Only then can you exploit them fully.

But the star of the hyperinflation collection, if I may so put it, is undoubtedly the Zimbabwean note for fifty trillion Zimbabwean dollars. I could have had the hundred trillion note, but I preferred the fifty for its cerulean colour—appropriate, considering that inflation in Zimbabwe had long since gone through the roof.

There was a reason why I preferred the blue note: I also possess a Zimbabwean $2 note dated 1986, when two such dollars would actually have bought you something. What is interesting (to me, at any rate) is that the design is almost exactly the same, $2 and $50,000,000,000,000. Indeed, the $2 of 1986 is the same design as that of 1975, when Zimbabwe was still Rhodesia. The Rhodesian coat of arms was removed, but apart from that, the design was more or less kept constant.

This, I think, is illustrative or symbolic of, the deep ambivalence felt in the country towards its colonial past, in some ways hated but in other ways admired, with a desire also for emulation and to keep some things the same. The uniforms, the judicial robes, Mr Mugabe's personal tailoring, are all indicative of the same thing; and it seems to me that if only we had taken Mr Mugabe to our hearts, or at least pretended to do so, to treat him not as an African potentate but as an English gentleman, much of Zimbabwe's hardship could have been avoided. If only our leaders had had the Ataturk penetration to a weak spot, how much better things might have been. But I suppose such an accommodation of vanity would not have met with everyone's approval.

The Governor of the Bank of Zimbabwe promises to pay the bearer on demand the sum of fifty trillion dollars: I admit that I cannot read those words without them bringing a smile to my face. It brings an absurd image to my mind, that of a teller of the Bank counting out fifty trillion dollars one by one. But of the course the paper on which the note is printed is now worth even more than fifty trillion times a single Zimbabwean dollar, something like a thousand trillion times, in fact. No matter how many times I read the words, they never fail to amuse me.

The Tyrant and the Hyperinflation collections are on my kitchen wall. I examine them closely while I wait for something to boil. They always tell me something new, like a great work of art.

Lightning Source UK Ltd.
Milton Keynes UK
UKOW04f0301200715

255465UK00001B/45/P

9 781943 003020